HOW TO GET ALONG
WITH OTHERS
USING COMMON SENSE
AND ANCIENT
HINDU WISDOM

A Practical Guide to Trouble-Free Living

Books by Swami Bhaskarananda

The Essentials of Hinduism : A Comprehensive Overview of the World's Oldest Religion

Meditation, Mind and Patanjali's Yoga : A Practical Guide to Spiritual Growth for Everyone

Life in Indian Monasteries : Reminiscences about Monks of the Ramakrishna Order

Reminiscences of Swami Brahmananda : The Mind-born Son of Sri Ramakrishna

The Philosophical Verses of Yogavāsishtha : An English Translation of Yogavāsishtha-sāra with Commentary and Sanskrit Text

The Wonder that is Srī Rāmakrishna : An English Translation of Srī Srī Rāmakrishna-Mahimā by Akshaykumār Sen

Journey from Many to One : Essentials of Advaita Vedanta

Ordering Information:
Viveka Press
2716 Broadway Ave E
Seattle, Washington 98102-3909
206-323-1228
vivekapress@vedanta-seattle.org

HOW TO GET ALONG WITH OTHERS USING COMMON SENSE AND ANCIENT HINDU WISDOM

A Practical Guide to Trouble-Free Living

by

Swami Bhaskarananda

Viveka Press

Seattle

Viveka Press, Seattle 98102

For more information write to:
Viveka Press
2716 Broadway Avenue East
Seattle, WA 98102-3909 USA
Phone: (206) 323-1228
Email: vivekapress@vedanta-seattle.org
http://www.vedanta-seattle.org/

Published 2013
Printed in the United States of America

Bhaskarananda, Swami.
How to get along with others using common sense and ancient Hindu wisdom : a practical guide to trouble-free living / by Swami Bhaskarananda.

ISBN-13: 978-1-884852-15-2
ISBN-10: 1-884852-15-7

Library of Congress Control Number: 2013942175

Dedicated to the memory of

Swami Vivekananda

on the occasion of his 150th birth anniversary

SWAMI VIVEKANANDA
1863-1902

Contents

8 HOW TO GET ALONG WITH YOUR SPOUSE 37

List of Illustrations

Cover photo by Devra Freedman

Preface

Getting along with others is not easy because there is no constancy in human behavior. The same person behaves differently at different times. We see fluctuations in human moods and temperaments and often wonder why such fluctuations happen. Thinkers, both ancient and modern, have tried to solve this mystery. For example, the ancient Hindu sage Kapila, who is the founder of the *Sankhya* school of Hindu philosophy, solved this mystery by interpreting human behavior in terms of *guna*s. This book is written mainly to acquaint the readers with this ancient philosophical term *guna* and how its clear concept can help us to master the art of getting along with all kinds of people.

In the publication of this book the following persons have helped immensely, and I acknowledge their loving assistance with deep gratitude.

Allen R. Freedman, Ph. D., for computer typesetting the manuscript.

Charles Mathias, Betsy Mathias and their daughter Laura for their valuable suggestions.

Devra A. Freedman and Allen R. Freedman for proofreading and editing.

I shall feel greatly rewarded if this book proves to be helpful to those for whom it is intended.

Swami Bhaskarananda
October, 2013

CHAPTER 1

INTRODUCTION

Why do our moods change so frequently?

At one time or the other we all have wondered: "Why is it so difficult to get along with people?" The answer to this question is that there is no constancy in human behavior. The same individual behaves differently at different times. Sometimes he is alert, calm, clear-minded, humble, nonviolent, sympathetic, understanding, loving and compassionate. At other times he is restless, energetic, power loving, domineering and egotistic. Still at another time he may be lethargic, dull and confused and senselessly cruel. No wonder it is so difficult to interact or get along with others.

If we think a little deeply we shall discover that we are more our minds than our bodies. The changing moods noticed in our behavior are mainly due to the changing states of our minds. The body may sometimes influence the mind, but most of the functions of the body are inspired by our thoughts, whether those thoughts belong to the conscious or the subconscious level of the mind. Hinduism considers reincarnation a fact. Therefore, according to Hinduism, what we call reflex action is also the outcome of repeated past actions of the body prompted by our thoughts of either this life or our previous lives.

One naturally wonders about the causes for the frequent fluctuations in human moods and temperaments. Many thinkers, both Eastern and Western,[1] have tried to solve this mystery. It seems some ancient thinkers of India were able to effectively and exhaustibly resolve this mystery.

---

1. For example, the Greek physician and writer Galen (circa 2nd century A.D.) claimed that all people were choleric (irritable), melancholy (sad/depressed), sanguine (cheerful/hopeful), or phlegmatic (calm). Dr. William H. Sheldon (1898-1977) classified human personality into three types according to their temperaments as (1) relaxed or internally calm, (2) energetic and (3) restrained.

CHAPTER 2

THE ANCIENT HINDU SAGE KAPILA'S METHOD OF INTERPRETING HUMAN BEHAVIOR WITH THE HELP OF THE *GUNAS*

To resolve the mystery about the causes for the frequent fluctuations in human moods and temperaments we shall take the help of the ancient Hindu sage Kapila, the founder of the *Sankhya* system of Hindu religious philosophy. According to *Sankhya* philosophy, the world has two parts: spirit and matter.

The spiritual domain of the world contains innumerable sentient entities, each one infinite and perfect. Such an entity is called a *purusha*.

The material domain of the world has its source in *prakriti* or Mother Nature, from which this entire material world has evolved.

Prakriti is insentient. It does not have consciousness.[2] Both *purusha* and *prakriti* are infinite and eternal.

Purusha is the sentient Spirit while *prakriti* is primordial matter. *Prakriti* is the finest form of matter that we can ever conceive of, and it is composed of three extremely subtle substances, each of which is called a *guna*. The Sanskrit word *guna* has more than one meaning. Usually it means *quality*. But in the context of *Sankhya* philosophy it means a strand or a thread. *Prakriti* is like a rope made of three strands. Each of these strands is called a *guna* in Sanskrit.

These three *guna*s are (1) *sattwa-guna* (also spelled *sattva-guna*), (2) *rajo-guna* and (3) *tamo-guna*.

Sattwa-guna is light or buoyant, bright or illuminating. It is of the nature of pleasure or joy; and it has the ability to reveal or make things known. The luminosity of light, the ability of the mind and the senses to know things, the reflecting power of a mirror, and the transparency of glass and crystals are all due to the presence of

---

2. It is necessary to understand the difference between the words "conscience" and "consciousness." Conscience is a function of the mind that enables you to know whether your actions are right or wrong. According to Hindu philosophy, it is a function of *buddhi* or intellect. On the other hand, consciousness of the mind is a state of awareness of the mind. Consciousness, however, is not an inherent quality of the mind. Mind is a subtle form of primordial matter or *prakriti*. And *prakriti* in its original state does not have consciousness inherent in it. Borrowing consciousness from *purusha* it becomes conscious.

sattwa-guna in them. Similarly if we see happiness, contentment, satisfaction, joy or bliss in a mind, we should know that it is due to the presence of *sattwa-guna* in it. In the same manner the lightness or buoyancy of cork or similar substances can be explained in terms of the presence of *sattwa-guna* in each of them.

Rajo-guna causes activity, movement and restlessness. These characteristics noticed in human beings or other objects and things indicate the presence of *rajo-guna* in them. Similarly, when we notice in our mind avarice, hankering, anger, egoism, vanity, and the wish to dominate over others, we should know that it is due to the presence of *rajo-guna* in it. *Rajo-guna* is also of the nature of pain and suffering. It is the cause of all types of painful experiences. In this world wherever we see pain or suffering, we should know that it is due to the presence of *rajo-guna*.

The main characteristics of *tamo-guna* are inertia, passivity, sluggishness, heaviness and negativity. It resists activity or movement. It renders the mind incapable of knowing things clearly by making it sluggish. It causes mental confusion, depression, bewilderment and ignorance. It induces drowsiness and sleep. It also causes senseless anger. Heaviness of metals such as lead indicate the presence of *tamo-guna* in them.

Both *prakriti* and *purusha*, being eternal and infinite, are in close proximity of each other. Due to its close proximity to *purusha*, *prakriti* borrows consciousness from *purusha* and becomes conscious. It is very much like certain

5

kinds of metal acquiring magnetic power when placed very close to a powerful magnet. This kind of acquired magnetism is called induced magnetism in physics. It should be noted here that even when this borrowed consciousness is present in *prakriti*, it does not really combine with *prakriti*. It is very much like the full moon being reflected on a mirror. Even though the reflected moon seems to be present in the mirror, it has not become one with the mirror. It has not become an inseparable part of *prakriti*. Aside from this, *purusha* is Spirit and the opposite of matter. So *purusha*, being Spirit, can never become one with *prakriti*, which is primordial matter.

Thus borrowing consciousness, *prakriti* starts evolving. Through a process of evolution it becomes this entire creation consisting of all kinds of fine and gross matter. Therefore, *prakriti* can also be called Mother Nature. One may wonder how *prakriti*, which is the finest of all kinds of matter, can evolve into gross material objects like rocks or stones. But we know that carbon dioxide, which is a formless gas, can become solid "dry ice." So also is the case with *prakriti*. Thus, all forms of gross or fine matter, and even energy and the mind, are only so many evolved forms of *prakriti*. Mind and energy, even though they are extremely fine, are no other than matter because they are the evolved forms of the primordial matter *prakriti*.

Since this world has evolved from *prakriti*, all human beings are a combination of *purusha* and *prakriti* or

Spirit and matter. Their physical bodies, energy, senses and minds are the evolved products of *prakriti*. The consciousness in them indicates the presence of *purusha* or the sentient Spirit in them. *Prakriti* being no other than the three *guna*s, all human beings have *sattwa-guna*, *rajo-guna* and *tamo-guna* in them.

According to *Sankhya* philosophy, when *purusha* is entangled with *prakriti* it is in a state of temporary bondage. While in bondage, *purusha* appears to forget its true nature and seems to suffer from limitations, such as pain and suffering, imposed on it by the *guna*s of *prakriti*. When *purusha* gets rid of this entanglement it becomes free from pain and suffering.

Since we all are a combination of *purusha* and *prakriti*, we are subject to suffering and pain. But when we become free from our entanglement with *prakriti*, our *purusha* nature becomes fully manifest. In other words, the Spirit becomes fully manifest. This is called spiritual liberation.

CHAPTER 3

HOW THE CHARACTERISTICS OF THE *GUNAS* MANIFEST IN PEOPLE

Some common characteristics of the *guna*s.

The *guna*s are like three siblings perpetually wrestling with one another. Each one wants to be prominent by subduing the other two. When one *guna* becomes predominant, its state of preponderance does not endure forever. Each of the other two subdued *guna*s tries to make itself prominent by subduing the other two. Therefore, in the same person *sattwa-guna*, *rajo-guna* and *tamo-guna* may become preponderant one after the other.

At the same time the *guna*s also cooperate with each another. It is like the cooperation of the wick, oil and the flame in an oil lamp. Even when *sattwa-guna* becomes predominant by subduing *rajo-guna* and *tamo-guna*, the two subdued *guna*s will still be associated with *sattwa-guna*, playing minor roles controlled by *sattwa-guna*.

As mentioned earlier, each of these *guna*s has its own characteristic qualities. The qualities of a particular *guna* become noticeably manifest when that *guna* becomes dominant after subduing the other two *guna*s.

9

Some characteristics of people with a preponderance of *sattwa-guna*.

The preponderance of *sattwa-guna* in human beings endows them with peacefulness of mind, purity of heart, happiness, joy, serenity, alertness, clarity of understanding, a natural tendency to be truthful, absence of anger, a natural tendency to renounce whatever is detrimental to spiritual life, kindness to all creatures, absence of backbiting, non-covetousness, gentleness, modesty, freedom from restlessness, spiritual vigor, a forgiving nature, absence of malice and haughtiness, the ability to understand the deeper significance of the scriptures, humility, unselfishness, sympathy, compassion, the spirit of nonviolence, and love of God. Higher spiritual truths become revealed to those who have a preponderance of *sattwa-guna*.

People with *sattwa-guna* prominent in them are fond of eating foods that are succulent, of smooth and creamy texture, substantial and agreeable. They like foods that augment life, cause strength, health, happiness, delight and firmness of mind. At the same time, they are fully aware that all the food that we eat is directly or indirectly connected with violence. For example, all food grains, such as rice, wheat, etc. have life in them. Had we sown them they would have developed into living plants. Eating them means destruction of all these life forms. Even honey is obtained by robbing the bees of the fruits of their hard labor. So also is the case with many other kinds of food that we consume. Such food cannot be considered pure or free from defects. Therefore, people with a preponderance of *sattwa-guna* mentally offer their food to God before eating, praying for its purification.

People with a preponderance of *sattwa-guna* naturally develop faith in God. In addition to that, if they try, the preponderance of *satta-guna* in them may enable them even to experience God. Such people endowed with an exuberance of *satta-guna* worship God with sincere love and devotion and gladly follow the injunctions of the scriptures. They do not make a show of their love and devotion to God. During worship they pray to God for the well being of all living beings. The purpose of their worship is to experience God and not to acquire mundane rewards or cheap occult powers.[3]

When they give gifts to people they do so with great kindness of heart. They give gifts only to deserving people, without expecting any kind of reciprocation, grati-

---

3. Divine incarnations like Sri Krishna, Gautama Buddha and Sri Ramakrishna have expressly stated that the use of occult powers by spiritual aspirants is detrimental to having spiritual enlightenment. Sri Krishna once said to his devotee and friend Uddhava, "For one who seeks union with Me (God), these (occult) powers have been called obstacles and things that cause waste of time." (*Uddhava Gita* 10/33). Buddha once forbade his disciples Pindola Bharadwaja and Moggallana to display occult power or iddhi as it is called in Buddhist literature. In *The Gospel of Sri Ramakrishna* we read that the Divine Mother showed him through a spiritual vision that occult powers are worthless, disgusting and despicable like human excreta. Such powers should, therefore, be carefully avoided by genuine seekers of spirituality.

tude or praise. It is mainly people with a preponderance of *sattwa-guna* who give gifts anonymously for noble causes without expecting any return.

Some characteristics of people with a preponderance of *rajo-guna*.

The preponderance of *rajo-guna* in people produces in them greed, avarice, restlessness and lack of satisfaction. They have a hankering for worldly things and are eager to get involved in all kinds of activity prompted by such hankering. They have lust, anger, arrogance, self-conceit, jealousy, envy, craving for name, fame, power and position, and the tendency to dominate others. They are also over-talkative. Such people can understand spiritual or scriptural teachings only superficially.

People with a preponderance of *rajo-guna* are generally fond of eating foods that are bitter, very sour, too salty, very spicy hot, pungent, dry and burning. Unfortunately, they have a tendency to eat mainly foods that are likely to eventually produce pain, sorrow and disease. People with a preponderance of *rajo-guna* easily get addicted to alcohol, tobacco and narcotics, even though from a medical point of view they are harmful to people's health.

In spite of all this, the preponderance of *rajo-guna* makes people very energetic and hyperactive, because among the three *guna*s, only *rajo-guna* has the principle of activity in things as well as people.

When people with a preponderance of *rajo-guna* perform a worship ritual, they do so to gain rewards in this life and in their after-life, such as curing an illness, getting more money, or going to heaven and having eternal enjoyment there. Sometimes their worship ritual is performed to get mainly name, fame, or praise from other people. It becomes more a display of their wealth than the devotional worship of God. Not only that, when they organize some family event, such as their daughter's marriage, they make a lavish display of their wealth to feel superior to others.

They think that they can buy spirituality by paying money. Once a very rich man came to a genuine holy man in India and saluted him after placing near the holy man's feet a bundle containing 100,000 rupees.

The holy man asked him, "What's this bundle for? What does it contain?"

"That's my humble gift to you, revered sir," replied the rich man, "this bundle contains 100,000 rupees."

As soon as the holy man heard this, he kicked the bundle away.

Feeling embarrassed, the rich man said, "Revered sir, you won't find too many devotees who can give you a gift of 100,000 rupees!"

"You won't find too many *sadhus* (holy men) either who can kick away 100,000 rupees," calmly replied the holy man. It should perhaps be mentioned here that genuine holy people are completely free from the craving for money, name, fame, power and position.

People with a preponderance of *rajo-guna* are also easily attracted to false prophets and charlatans. Only a person with a preponderance of *sattwa-guna* most of the time can recognize a genuine saint. Unfortunately, false prophets and charlatans are quite numerous. As long as genuine diamonds are considered precious, there will be imitation diamonds in circulation. Similarly, as long as genuine saints and prophets are greatly adored by people, there will surely be many charlatans impersonating genuine saints. Over 2,000 years ago even Jesus Christ cautioned his followers saying, "Beware of false prophets!"

When people with a preponderance of *rajo-guna* give gifts to others they always do so for selfish gain, expecting reciprocation from the recipients. In order to get fame, they may create endowments in universities or charitable organizations, either in their own names or jointly in the names of their spouses and themselves. They give donations to political parties with the sole intent of getting favors in return. They never give gifts selflessly or anonymously. Sometimes, out of a sense of obligation, they give gifts grudgingly.

Some characteristics of people with a preponderance of *tamo-guna*.

The preponderance of *tamo-guna* in people makes them lethargic, confused, depressed and sleepy. At the same time it can sometimes make them lustful, senselessly angry or violent. Such people can easily be incited to create riots and cause senseless killing of innocent people in the name of religion or anything else.

People with a preponderance of *tamo-guna* are unable to understand the deeper significance of the scriptures. It is mainly these people with a preponderance of *tamo-guna* who harm the world by misinterpreting the noble teachings of the scriptures.

People with a preponderance of *tamo-guna* are fond of eating foods that were cooked hours earlier, foods that are partially or fully rotten, malodorous and stale. Like the people with a preponderance of *rajo-guna*, those who are dominated by *tamo-guna* also are easily addicted to tobacco, alcohol and narcotics, even though all these substances are harmful to health. As mentioned earlier, according to Hinduism, no food is free from defects judging by how we procure it. For example, all edible plants, food grains, fish, birds and animals have life in them. To eat them we have to destroy their lives. As mentioned earlier, even when we procure honey, which is lifeless, we do that by robbing the bees of the fruits of their hard labor. Therefore, before eating or drinking any kind of food, Hindus are expected to mentally or ritually offer their food to God for its purification.

People with a preponderance of *tamo-guna*, however, lack this kind of thinking. Therefore, they do not mind eating food that has not been offered to God.

In this connection it should be mentioned here that people with a preponderance of *sattwa-guna* will have a natural dislike for the kinds of food that are liked by people with a preponderance of *tamo-guna* or *rajo-guna*.

People in whom *tamo-guna* is preponderant give gifts without judging whether the recipient deserves the gifts or if the gifts will harm the recipient.

Those with a preponderance of *tamo-guna* are easily attracted to false prophets and are vulnerable to charlatans pretending to be saints. They want to know whether these so-called prophets can cure illnesses or perform magic in the name of religion.

People with a preponderance of *tamo-guna* also lack common sense and the faculty of discrimination.

Only one *guna* can be preponderant at any given point in time.

At any given point in time, only one of these three *gunas* can be preponderant in a person's body and mind. Depending upon which *guna* is preponderant, the characteristics of that particular *guna* will become manifest in that person at that time.

Who is a *sattwik* person?

When *sattwa-guna* is preponderant in a person *most of the time*, he or she is called a *sattwik* person (closest English pronunciation: sutt-wick). And the kind of food a *sattwik* person is fond of eating is called *sattwik* food.

Who is a *rajasik* person?

When *rajo-guna* is predominant in a person *most of the time* he or she is called a *rajasik* person (closest English pronunciation: ra-jaw-sick). And the kind of food a *rajasik* person is fond of eating is called *rajasik* food.

Who is a *tamasik* person?

A person with preponderance of *tamo-guna most of the time* is called a *tamasik* person (closest English pronunciation: tum-awe-sick). And the kind of food a *tamasik* person is fond of eating is called *tamasik* food.

The preponderant *guna* can sometimes use one or more of the subdued *guna*s.

As mentioned earlier, when one *guna* becomes predominant by subduing the other two, the subdued *guna*s are not wiped out. Any one of these two *guna*s, even though subdued, can still be somewhat active under the control of the *guna* that is predominant at that time. For example, when *sattwa-guna* is predominant, it can use the subdued *rajo-guna* to perform some activity conducive to spiritual life. Thus, using *rajo-guna*, a person with a preponderance of *sattwa-guna* can engage in selfless activities such as giving food and shelter to the needy, or providing free medical treatment or education for indigent people.

It should be noted here that when *sattwik* people engage in philanthropic activities, they do so without any craving for name, fame, power and position. They do not

SRI RAMAKRISHNA (1836-1886)
IN SPIRITUAL ECSTACY

engage in such activities to attain personal glory. They perform them selflessly or as a service to God, looking upon those served as so many children of God.

Example of a *sattwik* person using his subdued *tamo-guna*.

In this context I would like to mention that Hinduism accepts only one God, and says that we are all God's *true* children. God does not have stepchildren. Nor can God have any adopted children because, in that case, we have to admit the existence of another Creator whose children have been adopted by God. According to Sri Ramakrishna (1836-1886), the great Hindu saint of the modern age, giving selfless service to people, looking upon them as children of God, is conducive to developing a *sattwik* mind (a mind which has a preponderance of *sattwa-guna most of the time*). Such a mind is also called a "pure" mind. According to Hinduism, the most ancient living faith in the world, it is this pure mind that enables a person to have God-vision. Jesus Christ echoes the same truth when he says, "Blessed are the pure in heart for they shall see God."

Sri Ramakrishna also talked about how *sattwa-guna*, when it is preponderant in a person, can use the subdued *tamo-guna* to enhance his or her spirituality. *Bhakti* or loving devotion to God is an endowment of *sattwa-guna*. Sometimes, out of an intense yearning for the vision of God, a spiritual aspirant may say demandingly to God, "God, you must show yourself to me! You have created

19

me. I am your child! Unless you show yourself to me, I shall cut my throat!" Sri Ramakrishna says that this attitude caused by an intense yearning for the vision of God is generated by *tamo-guna* inspired by *sattwa-guna*. This is a case where the preponderant *sattwa-guna* is using the subdued *tamo-guna* to help the spiritual aspirant achieve his or her spiritual goal.

In the life of Sri Ramakrishna we find a beautiful example of this phenomenon. In spite of his intense spiritual practice, Sri Ramakrishna, then a young priest in the temple of the Divine Mother Kali[4] in Dakhshineswar,

---

4. According to Hinduism, God transcends time, space and causation. Transcending time, God is eternal. Transcending space, God is infinite; and transcending the ceaseless chain of cause and effect, God is changeless. God being infinite is formless. Therefore, God is beyond personality and gender. God is neither father nor mother. Yet, when the finite human mind tries to think of God, it projects its limitations on God. As human beings cannot think other than in human terms, the first projection of the human mind on God is a human personality, no matter how glorified. This is how impersonal God appears to be a person to human beings. God appears to acquire a glorified human personality—but devoid of human limitations. At any given point in time a human being can exist occupying only the limited space that his or her body occupies, but God does not have that kind of limitation. God is omnipresent. A human being is limited in power, but God is omnipotent—all-powerful. A human being has only limited knowledge, but God is omniscient—all-knowing. Then again, some human beings who dearly love their fathers, project fatherhood on God. Similarly,

footnote continued on next page

was not yet able to get Her vision. So his yearning for God-vision became extremely intense. One day the excruciating pain of not having been able to get the vision of the Divine Mother became so unbearable that he cried to Her saying, "Mother, unless you show thyself to me, I shall cut my throat!" Then snatching the sword away from the hand of the basalt image of the Divine Mother Kali standing in front of him, he was about to cut his own throat. Immediately the Divine Mother appeared

---

some human beings, such as the Hindus, who love their mothers dearly, project motherhood on God. To them God appears to be a loving mother—the Divine Mother. Hindus clearly understand that "God the Father" and "God the Mother" are one and the same God.

If you look at the blue sky through a pair of red eyeglasses the sky will appear to be reddish. Then again, if you look at the same blue sky using a pair of green eyeglasses the sky will look greenish. The blue sky does not change its color. The red or green color is projected on the blue sky by the viewer's red or green eyeglasses. The reddish sky and the greenish sky are not different from each other. They are one and the same blue sky.

Human minds are like so many pairs of different colored eyeglasses. Some minds may project fatherhood on God while other minds may project motherhood on God. Hindus look upon God as father, mother, friend, child or even sweetheart, just in order to feel close to God using their feeling of love. At the same time, they are fully aware that these are only so many projections of their minds on the one and only God. The *Rigveda,* the most ancient scripture of Hinduism, teaches that God is one; only different sages call the same God by various names.

before him in all Her Divine splendor and stopped him! This is how Sri Ramakrishna attained God-vision using his subdued *tamo-guna* inspired by his *sattwa-guna*.

CHAPTER 4

HINDU PSYCHOLOGY EXPLAINS WHAT THE MIND IS

Knowledge of Hindu psychology can be helpful in getting along with people.

As mentioned earlier, to get along with others, we have to remember that people's personalities depend more on their minds than their bodies. Therefore, some knowledge of Hindu psychology can be immensely helpful.

Unfortunately, Western psychology is not yet sure of what the mind is. As the joke goes, a Western psychologist was asked, "What's mind?" The psychologist replied, "No matter!" He was asked again, "What's matter?" Then he replied, "Never mind!" The joke conveys the message that the Western psychologists think that mind is not matter. Or they do not know what the mind is.

On the other hand, even in ancient times, Hindu sages like Kapila and Patanjali definitely knew that mind, being an evolved product of *prakriti*, was no other than matter, even though extremely fine matter.

What we commonly call the *mind*—the medium with the help of which we know things—is called in Hindu psychology the *antahkaranam*. The Sanskrit word *antahkaranam* literally means "the inner instrument for acquiring knowledge" (*antah*=inner; *karanam*=instrument).

The same *antahkaranam*, however, is given different names depending on the various functions it preforms.

Let us suppose I become aware of an object seen at a distance, but I am unable to see it clearly because it is surrounded by mist. My *antahkaranam* cognizes the object but is unable to determine what it really is. "Is it the stump of a tree or a standing grizzly bear?" I wonder. When the *antahkaranam* has this kind of vacillating cognition, it is given the name *manas*. As there is no exact equivalent of the word *manas* in English, it is inadequately translated as "mind."

The *antahkaranam* is given the name *buddhi* when it uses its determinative faculty to decisively determine the true character of the cognized object, and thus acquires the non-vacillating knowledge that the object cannot be a large grizzly bear, because this is the time of year when bears hibernate. Therefore, it is definitely the stump of a tree. In the absence of an exact English counterpart of the Sanskrit word *buddhi*, it is inadequately translated into English as "intellect."

The *antahkaranam* is given the name *chitta* when it functions as memory and remembrance.

When someone's *antahkaranam* makes him or her aware of being an individual different from everything and everyone else, then the *antahkaranam* is called the ego or *ahankara*. This ego is a factor of separation. It separates a person from every other person or thing.

It should, however, be remembered that the *antahkaranam*, which is inadequately translated into English as *mind*, is also composed of the three *gunas* of *prakriti* because, according to Hinduism, everything belonging to this entire universe is an evolved product of *prakriti*. And *prakriti* being primordial matter composed of the three *gunas*, *antahkaranam*, which is also matter, is composed of the three *gunas—sattwa-guna, rajo-guna* and *tamo-guna*.

CHAPTER 5

HOW A *TAMASIK* PERSON CAN BE TRANSFORMED INTO A *SATTWIK* PERSON

A *tamasik* person cannot directly be transformed into a *sattwik* person. First such a person has to try to be *rajasik*. Only then he can gradually come up to the sattwik level. He should first get involved in brisk mental and physical activity to create a state of a preponderance of *rajo-guna*. For example, he could start playing a vigorous game of tennis. This will bring his mind and body up to the *rajasik* level. Thereafter, while resting, he could listen to some soothing music, preferably of a spiritual nature. While listening to that music his mind will gradually become calm, indicating that it has become *sattwik*. Or, he could read some inspiring religious literature, such as a well-written biography of a genuine saint or prophet. While reading such a book, his mind will gradually become calm and serene, having been inspired by the calm and serene personality of the saint or the prophet. Also if he has been taught how to meditate by a genuine teacher, meditation may help him to gradually make his mind calm and serene.

In this context I would like to mention a case in point. But I should first mention that I belong to a global Hindu monastic Order called the Ramakrishna Order. It is the monastic wing of the well-known Hindu religious organization in India called the Ramakrishna Mission.[5] At any given point in time we have quite a few novices (called *brahmacharis*) in our Order who are going through spiritual training under senior monks called *Swamis*. Once in a while a novice who is new to the monastery may be found to be depressed. Depression is a sign of the

5. The Ramakrishna Order is a global religious organization, with two separate branches rooted in the same spiritual ideology. The names of the branches are the "Ramakrishna Math" and the "Ramakrishna Mission." The Ramakrishna Math is a religious monastic order. It was set up by Swami Vivekananda to follow the teachings of Sri Ramakrishna. The Ramakrishna Math was registered as a trust in 1901. The Ramakrishna Math is headquartered at Belur Math (in West Bengal, India), and shares the location with the related organization, the Ramakrishna Mission. The Ramakrishna Mission, members of which are both lay and monastic followers of Sri Ramakrishna, is a philanthropic organization. The Ramakrishna Mission was also founded by Swami Vivekananda (1863-1902) on May 1, 1897. As the representative of Hinduism, the Swami had attended the historic Parliament of Religions held in Chicago in 1893 and turned out to be its star performer. He was the first one to preach Hinduism most effectively in the West. At the request of his American admirers, he was instrumental in founding the Vedanta Societies in New York as well as in San Antonio Valley in California. Now there are thirteen Vedanta Societies with their eight sub-centers in America. Swami Vivekananda (1836-1886), was also the foremost disciple of Sri Ramakrishna who is considered a Divine Incarnation by millions in India and abroad.

preponderance of *tamo-guna* in a person. Due to his depression the novice may not even want to leave his room. In such a case, the senior Swamis ask other novices to somehow coax the depressed monk to come out of his room and start doing vigorous physical exercise, such as doing spade work in the monastery garden. These physical activities will bring up the *tamasik* state of the novice's body and mind to the *rajasik* level. After that it will be possible for the novice to transform his *rajasik* state of body and mind into the *sattwik* state as explained in the preceding paragraph.

About fifty-three years ago, as a *brahmachari* (novice) I had to go through a two-year training program in the Training Center for *brahmacharis* at our Order's headquarters near the city of Calcutta in India. At that time one *brahmachari* who was undergoing training with us, started showing signs of being depressed. His depression became so bad that he could not be easily persuaded to leave his bed and come out of his room. We had to bring his food to his room because he felt that he didn't even have enough strength to go to the dining room. The authorities of our Order sent him to the large modern hospital that our Order runs in Calcutta. The doctors there could not find anything wrong with his physical health. So he was sent back to the branch center of our Order from which he had come to have training at the headquarters. That branch center was several hundred miles away from Calcutta and it ran eleven schools, including two high schools, as well as one large dormitory for boys.

Just eight or ten days later, we were surprised to hear the good news that the *brahmachari* had completely recovered from his depression and had even started playing volleyball with the boys in the dormitory.

The principal of the Training Center at our headquarters at that time was a saintly Swami with deep knowledge of human psychology and spiritual life. He explained to us that the depression of the *brahmachari* must have been caused by a sudden shock to his attitude toward God. He was a devotee of God endowed with a personality. But at the Training Center the trainees had lately been introduced to the *Advaita* philosophy, which speaks of God as the impersonal and formless Divine Reality that transcends time, space and causation. The idea of God devoid of any personality, as taught by *Advaita* philosophy, clashed with his idea of God endowed with a personality. This shock caused him great mental confusion and his mind became overpowered by *tamo-guna*.[6] But when he went back to the familiar environment of the center from which he had come to the headquarters for training, his mind gradually recovered from his shock. Getting involved in the daily activities of the center and also in occasional brisk activities, such as playing volleyball, helped him to recover from his depression. *Tamoguna* was no longer preponderant in his body and mind. Then he was able to do his daily meditation and his mind

6. One of the characteristics of *tamo-guna* is that it causes confusion in the mind of a person. [Please see page 14 to know the characteristics of people with a preponderance of *tamo-guna*.]

became calm, serene and cheerful, indicating that it had again acquired a state of preponderance of *sattwa-guna*. After a few months, he returned to the headquarters and completed his training. By that time he had also come to understand that God may appear to be either personal or impersonal depending upon the mental attitude of the spiritual aspirant.

CHAPTER 6

BASICS OF HOW TO GET ALONG WITH OTHERS

To be able to get along with others you should have a good understanding of the *guna*s.

Every individual is a package of the body, mind, energy and the senses. This package is also called "the body-mind complex." This package is none other than an evolved product of *prakriti* or primordial matter. At the same time, this package has consciousness associated with it. As mentioned earlier, this consciousness has been borrowed by *prakriti* from *purusha*, which is the only source of consciousness. Consciousness or *purusha* does not change. It is only *prakriti* that evolves or undergoes change. *Prakriti* is composed of three *guna*s: *sattwa-guna*, *rajo-guna* and *tamo-guna*. As mentioned above, human beings who are so many evolved products of *prakriti*, are composed of *sattwa-guna*, *rajo-guna* and *tamo-guna*. [In this connection please read "The ancient Hindu sage Kapila's method of interpretation of human behavior" on page 3.]

Your behavior with others must relate to three factors: time, place and other people's personalities.

To interact properly with other people, you have to consider three factors: time, place and the personality of a person.

Behavior appropriate at one time may not at all be appropriate at another time. For example, one's behavior at the time of a friend's marriage and when the friend is terminally ill should not be the same. Then again, the kind of behavior that is proper at a place of festivity, may not at all be proper in a different place, such as in a funeral procession.

Similarly, the kind of behavior that is proper in dealing with a child will not be proper in regard to an adult. The behavior that is proper in regard to a classmate will surely not be the right behavior in regard to a highly respected person, such as a highly revered saint.

Before learning how to get along with others, you have to first learn to get along with your closest companion—your own mind.

Charity begins at home. Before learning how to get along with others, you have to learn how to get along with your own mind. To judge other people *correctly*, you need a calm and serene state of mind. In other words, you should for the time being create a state of a preponderance of *sattwa-guna* in your mind. Otherwise your judgment of others will not be correct.

CHAPTER 7

HOW TO GET ALONG WITH *SATTWIK*, *RAJASIK* AND *TAMASIK* PEOPLE

How to get along with *sattwik* people or people who have a preponderance of *sattwa-guna* in them most of the time.

It is very easy to get along with *sattwik* people. They are the cream of human society. They are the best. They have calm, serene and cheerful minds. They have a clearer and deeper understanding of everything. They are unselfish, kind, and compassionate. Their minds are naturally attuned to high idealism. As they do not crave praise, they cannot be flattered. As they are free from greed, they cannot be bribed. [To know more about them see "Some characteristics of people with a preponderance of *sattwa-guna*" on page 10.]

How to get along with *rajasik* people or people who have a preponderance of *rajo-guna* in them most of the time.

Getting along with *rajasik* people is not as easy as to get along with *sattwik* people. *Rajasik* people have preponderance of *rajo-guna*. *Rajo-guna* causes energy.

Therefore, *rajasik* people are very energetic. They are extremely eager to have objects of sense enjoyment, money, power and position. If others create obstacles to their achieving all this, they become angry.[7] They have a natural tendency to dominate over others. They love praise and flattery. They can be very talkative. If you surrender to them they will protect you. But if you oppose them they will fight you tooth and nail and, if possible, try to destroy you. [To know more about them see "Some characteristics of people with preponderance of *rajo-guna*" on page 12]

How to get along with *tamasik* people or people who have a preponderance of *tamo-guna* in them most of the time.

It is also not easy to get along with *tamasik* people. Since *tamasik* people have a preponderance of *tamo-guna* in them, they are usually lethargic and confused. They frequently suffer from depression. As their thinking is not clear, they can be senselessly cruel. It is hard for such people to understand or accept higher ideals of life. They are extremely body-minded. They are driven by their physical urges more than anything else. [To know more about them see "Some characteristics of people with pre-ponderance of *tamo-Guna*" on page 14]

---

7. *Kama esha krodha esha rajoguna-samudbhava*, *The Bhagavadgita* 3/37—Desire for objects of sense enjoyment and (consequent) anger are born out of *rajo-guna*.

CHAPTER 8

HOW TO GET ALONG WITH YOUR SPOUSE

(a) How to get along with your spouse.

Once a young man came to an elderly householder in India seeking advice. The young man was going to be married shortly. He asked the elderly gentleman, "Sir, what's the secret of a happy marriage?"

The elderly gentleman replied, "I have to take the help of an analogy to tell you the secret. Consider a newly married couple in America. On their honeymoon they went to the island state of Hawaii and decided to go to an uncrowded beach and spend some time together undisturbed by others.

"It was summer and their car didn't have air conditioning. In search of a secluded beach they drove for several hours. At last they found an idyllic, small beach where there was no one around. They were exhausted after driving all those hours. They parked their car, and taking out a blanket from the car, spread it out on the sand. Then simultaneously similar thoughts came to their minds.

"The husband thought, 'Wouldn't it be nice if I can put my head on my wife's lap and rest for a while?' The wife also thought that it would be nice if she could put her head on her husband's lap and rest."

Then the gentleman said, " In such a situation, you can easily see that it is not possible for both to have their wishes fulfilled at the same time. One of them has to make self-sacrifice for the other spouse to make him or her happy. Young man, marriage is such a relationship. The spouses should make willing and loving self-sacrifice for each other to make themselves happy.

"Then again, who is a good husband? The husband who makes willing and loving self-sacrifice for his wife is a good husband. The same is true for a good wife."

The gentleman ended by saying, "This is the secret of a happy marriage. This is the secret of how to enjoy marital bliss! But you may argue and say, 'If one spouse goes on making self-sacrifice and the other one doesn't, then how can there be happiness in married life?' The answer to this question is that the spouse who makes such willing and loving self-sacrifice, will surely be able to make the other spouse happy. And having been able to make him or her happy, the self-sacrificing spouse will find great happiness.

"For example, mothers take care of their newly-born babies 24 hours a day. The babies don't give thanks to their mothers even once for the loving care they get from them. Nor do they give any kind of service in return to their mothers. Yet the mothers find great joy in unilaterally giving all kinds of loving service to their babies. You may say, 'Mothers find joy in taking care of their babies because the babies are their own. They have a sense of ownership in regard to their own babies. They don't have similar feelings in regard to other women's babies.' The argument against what you are saying is that a similar feeling of ownership can be there between spouses as well. In regard to his or her spouse every husband or wife also thinks, 'He or she is my very own.'"

(b) How to get along with your wife in different situations.

(*i*) **General rules about how to get along with your wife:** You should always treat your wife with much love and gratitude. Unfortunately, since the olden days, societies in the world have been more or less male-dominated.

(*ii*) **How to get along with a moody wife:** A very knowledgeable lady, a renowned physician in England, told her niece, whom I knew, "Most women, particularly in middle age, due to hormonal deficiency suffer from frequent fluctuations in their emotions." Therefore, unless your wife is an exception, you should expect that your wife's moods are likely to change frequently. You should study her moods and act accordingly.

If she is sad without any valid reason, try to cheer her up by doing what may make her happy. Gifts are tokens of love and affection. You can give her a gift. That may make her happy. One very experienced, elderly protestant Christian minister of America said, "It is always better to give gifts to your wife when she least expects it. It goes without saying that you must never forget to give her gifts on her birthday or on your marriage anniversary. But giving her a surprise gift when she least expects it will surely delight her more."

The wives naturally expect their husbands to love them more dearly than others. Therefore, every husband should make it obvious to his wife that she is the dearest and most important person in his life.

In this world, unfortunately, many women are treated unfairly. A typical example of this you may find in chapter 8 of St. John's Gospel in the New Testament. According to this Gospel, some scribes and Pharisees came to Jesus with a woman, surrounded by a frenzied crowd. Jesus was sitting on the ground at that time. The woman reportedly had committed adultery and was therefore to be stoned to death according to Jewish law. Then the Pharisees asked Jesus if the woman should be given that punishment according to the law given by Moses. Without looking at them and still sitting on the ground, Jesus said, "Let one who has not committed any sin be the first one to cast a stone at her."

After hearing his words, having been pricked by their own conscience, one by one all the accusers left that place. Then Jesus asked that woman, "Where are those accusers? Has no one condemned you?" She said, "No Lord, no one has condemned me!" Then Jesus said to her, "I don't condemn you either. Go, and don't commit sin anymore."

This Biblical story is significant because you can see in it how injustice was done to women even at that early period in history. Adultery cannot be done by anyone unilaterally. Two persons—a man and a woman—are involved in an act of adultery. But in this story we see that only the woman was being punished, and not the man! The story also reveals Jesus' sense of fairness and compassion.

Far away from that period, even in today's societies women are sometimes humiliated and discriminated against. Therefore, as a husband, you should try to reassure your wife that whether others treat her fairly or not, she is the dearest and the most perfect companion in your life. You must make her feel that she is the queen in your family.

You must make sure that she doesn't have to bear the entire load of her domestic duties, such as cooking, cleaning, etc. As you are her life's partner, it should be your duty to share with her all those responsibilities. In some families, such as those in countries like India, husbands never enter the kitchen except to eat; they don't usually take part in any culinary activity. Such practice shows lack of consideration, and is not at all fair to the women.

(*iii*) **How to get along with your wife who is very much attached to her parents:** It is natural for good sons and daughters to love and respect their parents. But unfortunately they may not have the same feelings toward their in-laws. This may cause some problems between husbands and wives. If your wife is very much attached to her own parents, for the sake of maintaining peace in your family you must not object to her behavior. In such a situation you should play an impartial role and give loving behavior to both yours as well as your wife's parents. Whenever the occasions demand, you must make sure that both your parents and your wife's parents get similar gifts from you. You should also remember that since your wife's parents love her, it is natural for them to love you also as their daughter's husband.

(*iv*) **How to get along with your wife who has to take care of a baby or a toddler:** Taking care of babies and young children, such as toddlers, is not an easy job. Once a member of our church (temple) left her three-year-old grandson with me for about an hour. As I was the youngest child of my parents I didn't have to take care of any younger brother or sister in my premonastic life. As a result, I was not used to babysitting. After taking care of that little boy for half an hour or so, I felt totally exhausted. Then my respect for mothers increased all the more. Therefore, I would advise you to have special sympathy and appreciation for your wife who has to take care of a baby or a young child. If you don't have the experience of babysitting you should learn how to do it and try to help your wife whenever you can. Also to lighten the burden of her daily household chores you should take over some of her duties. Otherwise, if you are financially capable, employ someone to help your wife to perform those household chores.

(*v*) **How to get along with your wife who has developed an incurable disease:** When a couple gets married in a church or temple, both the spouses have to take the oath in the presence of God that they won't leave each other until death separates them. Yet it is often seen that spouses break their vows and divorce each other. I read a sad story about a relatively young married couple in America. Both of them were engineers. Unfortunately, the wife, who was not even thirty, got Lou Gehrig's disease. This disease is considered incurable. So her husband divorced her and married some other woman. It is a shame that he left her when his wife needed him most! There is no doubt that the husband was selfish and only cared for himself. Such tendencies are the signs of a person who is *rajasik* by nature. Had he been of a *sattwik* temperament he would never have abandoned his wife and would have taken good care of her.

In my life I have seen several husbands, mostly from India, who never left their wives who were suffering from incurable diseases. With great love and sympathy they stood by their wives and took care of them. One such husband was an immigrant in Canada. He had two grown up daughters who were born in Canada. They advised their father to put their mother in a nursing home. But he didn't do that. He kept her at home, arranged for all her nursing and medical care there. He didn't want to send her away from the loving home environment she was used to. He told me that before she had her incurable illness he had lived many happy years together with his wife and was extremely grateful to her for that. Aside from that, as the scriptures of Hinduism dictate, he felt that he should be an ideal husband and stand by his wife in times of both pain and pleasure. Therefore, he couldn't even think of hurting her feelings by sending her to a nursing home! The moral of this true story is for husbands to learn how to lovingly get along with their wives who are suffering from incurable diseases.

(*vi*) **How to get along with your wife who has been harshly treated by someone:** Once a member of our church came to see me with his gentle and very good-natured six-year-old daughter, and said, "Swami, she wants to ask you a question." When I asked her what her question was, she said, "In school, when I was standing, a girl came and pushed me. What should I do?" I told her, "You don't have to do anything to her. Pray to God and say, 'God, please make her a good girl. Don't let her push anyone any more!'"

If your wife has been harshly treated by someone, you should give her similar advice. In this world there are all kinds of people. Some are *sattwik,* while others are either *rajasik* or *tamasik.* They act having been influenced by the *guna* that is preponderant in them. No matter how much you may want, you can't change them unless they change themselves. If your wife feels that she has been harshly treated by someone, it is best for her to ignore that. Otherwise, if she goes on meditating on the harsh behavior of that other person her misery will only be prolonged. In Hinduism the Vedas teach people to overcome anger by creating an opposite feeling in the mind.[8] Similarly, hurt feelings can be overcome by either love or a prayer to God asking Him to change the nature of those who hurt us.

(c) How to get along with a *sattwik* wife.

If the wife is of *sattwik* nature her husband should be considered extremely lucky. In fact, a *sattwik* wife is a spiritual blessing to her husband. Such a wife in Hindu tradition is called a *sahadharmini*—a co-partner in spiritual life. A *sattwik* wife has all the wonderful characteristics of *sattwa-guna* manifested in her. She is endowed with a peaceful mind, purity of heart, happiness, joy, serenity, alertness, clarity of understanding, a natural tendency to be truthful, absence of anger, a natural tendency to renounce whatever is detrimental to spiritual life, kindness to all creatures, absence of the habit of back-biting, non-covetousness, gentleness, modesty, freedom from restlessness, a forgiving nature, absence of malice

---

8. *Akrodhen krodham—Sama Veda.*

and haughtiness, the ability to understand the deeper significance of the scriptures, humility, unselfishness, sympathy, compassion, the spirit of nonviolence, and love of God. The company of such a wife will surely help the husband grow spiritually.

A beautiful example of such a *sattwik* wife we find in Sri Sarada Devi, the saintly wife of Sri Ramakrishna, considered one of the greatest Hindu saints of this age. They were married, but their marriage was never consummated. Theirs was a purely spiritual marriage.

Following the tradition that existed in India more than 150 years ago, Sri Sarada Devi was married in her childhood. After attaining puberty, she left her parents' home and came to live with her husband.

Sri Ramakrishna asked her, "Have you come to drag me down to a life of worldliness?"

Sri Sarada Devi, the most wonderful *sattwik* wife that she was, replied, "No, I have come to help you in your spiritual life."

This is how this wonderful couple spent their married life together. By their own admission, they always saw the presence of divinity in each other. Sri Ramakrishna never took his wife on a pleasure trip. He hardly gave her any worthwhile gift except a pair of golden bangles, which was paid for by one of his admirers. It is also a fact that being a saint, he was under a vow of poverty and didn't have any money or property. He lived in a room in

SRI SARADA DEVI
1853-1920

a large temple complex dedicated to the Divine Mother Kali and owned by Rani Rasmani, one of his admirers. Rani Rasmani's son-in-law Mathur, who managed the temple complex, was very much devoted to Sri Rama- krishna and took care of most of his day-to-day financial needs.

Sri Sarada Devi, like an ideal Hindu wife, served her husband with all her heart and soul. She used to live in a tiny room in the same temple complex close to Sri Ramakrishna's room. Devotees would frequently come to have the holy company of the saint. In addition to doing her various household chores, Sri Sarada Devi used to cook for her husband and also those devotees who would sometimes stay overnight in Sri Ramakrishna's room. Being of pure *sattwik* nature, she never complained or demanded anything mundane from her saintly husband, and felt extremely happy in just being able to serve him. After the passing away of Sri Ramakrishna, she said to a devotee, "As long as he was alive, the pitcher of my heart was always full of spiritual joy and bliss!"

Sri Ramakrishna used to call the women of *sattwik* na- ture *vidya-shakti*. According to him, such women help their husbands to go towards God. Manu, the ancient sage and lawgiver of Hinduism, said, "Where women are adored or worshipped, there the gods are delighted; but where they are not adored or worshipped, all religious ceremonies become futile and useless."[9] It is not diffi-

---

9. *See Manusamhita* 3/56.

cult to presume that when Manu made this statement he must have had such *sattwik* women in mind.

It is obvious that to get along with a wife who has a *sattwik* nature is not hard at all.

(d) How to get along with a *rajasik* wife.

If your wife is of *rajasik* nature she will be ambitious, talkative and domineering. To please her, you should give her complete freedom to make all the decisions in regard to your household. You must not contradict her when she is talking. Give her the freedom to talk. When she is talking develop the habit of saying to her, "Yes, dear!" as often as you can. "Yes, dear!" is a great mantra; it always works! If you use it frequently, your family peace will not be disturbed. I have seen the husbands of two apparently happily married couples who use this mantra as frequently as possible.

Once three business executives in Seattle were having coffee together in their office canteen and chitchatting about their family life. One of them said humorously, "I have a very happy marriage because my wife and I believe in the division of labor. My wife makes all household decisions, such as which house or furniture to buy, what improvements should be made to the kitchen, bedrooms, etc. And I decide what the foreign policy of our country should be!"

That gentleman was right about his behavior with his wife because most *rajasik* women consider their homes their nests. They want to be queens of their nests. This is why most married women, especially in the West, don't want to live with their mothers-in-law. Aside from this, they don't want anyone to interfere with the way they take care of their nests.

Once I met an American bishop of the Lutheran church on a ship. The captain of the ship was a gentleman from India. The captain's wife also happened to be on that ship. She was then living with her husband in the captain's quarters. Her husband brought her along with him to show her America. The bishop, curious to know about family life in India, was asking her many questions. Thus he came to know that she lived in her home in Bombay with her in-laws. The bishop asked her if living with her in-laws was comfortable for her. She replied, "I am very happy that they live with me. I feel just as close to them as to my own parents."

Hearing that, the bishop said rather sadly, "I have a married daughter who has a baby son. While visiting her, my wife once gave her some advice about how she should take care of him. This displeased our daughter very much. So she said to her mother, 'Mom, you had your chance when I was a baby. Please don't interfere with how I take care of him!'"

Most men and women try to enhance their physical beauty in order to be attractive to others. That's why they use attractive clothes and other external decorations. This tendency is all the more pronounced in women. At one time I used to wonder why in India and other countries women have their ears and noses pierced to wear ornaments. To have your ears and noses pierced must be painful. Yet women don't mind going through such pain in order to be physically attractive to men. They also use nail polish, hair dye, lipstick and various other cosmetics in order to be attractive to men. Then it dawned on me that for the propagation of the human race, Mother Nature must have given them that urge to attract men.

If we look at flowering plants, we see a similar phenomenon. For cross-pollination flowers have to attract insects. That's why flowers have fragrance as well as nectar inside them to attract bees and other insects. For the same reason, day-blooming flowers have bright and radiant colors to attract insects, while night-blooming flowers are all white in order to be visible to insects in the darkness of the night. Nocturnal flowers also have a stronger fragrance to attract insects. This explains why women, like flowers, indulge in various physical decorations to attract men. Otherwise, the human race would have become extinct.

But this urge to attract men is only one aspect of their nature. The noblest aspect of a woman's character is manifested when she becomes a mother. Motherhood is her greatest glory. It is the mother who gives birth to babies. And when born, the babies get food to sustain them from the mother's body. She also most lovingly takes care of her baby 24 hours a day without caring for her own physical comfort. That's why, in the creation of progeny, mother's role is of supreme importance. Compared to her role, the role of a father is relatively of less importance. Among all forms of human love, mother's love is the most selfless. That's why the scriptures of Hinduism, such as the Upanishads, teach Hindus that they should look upon their mothers as God. Hinduism also teaches that mother and one's country of birth are superior to even heaven.

But the fact that women want to make themselves more beautiful by using cosmetics, ornaments, attractive clothes, etc., proves that they are not satisfied with their own natural looks. In other words, they must think that they are not as beautiful as they should be. The husbands, therefore, should reassure their wives frequently that they find them to be attractive. They should also learn to express their love for their wives in a manner that can be easily understood by them. Husbands should also praise their wives frequently. That will surely make them happy. Just about everyone, except those who are saintly, loves to be praised.

The husbands of *rajasik* wives should know that, among other things, their wives will crave positions of leadership. Aside from this, *rajasik* wives will be lustful, and they will have a tendency to become angry when they won't get what they want from their husbands.[10] They will be restless and will like to travel a lot.

---

10. "Lustfulness and anger arise from *rajo-guna*. It has insatiable appetite and is most sinful. Know it to be an enemy."—*The Bhagavadgita* 3/37.

Many years ago I happened to read a travelogue written by a *rajasik* lady. Her husband was a famous scientist. On invitation he had to visit different countries. During those trips he took his *rajasik* wife along with him. The travelogue, which she wrote, was full of descriptions of restaurants, parties and various kinds of shows, parks, etc. She didn't write at all about the history, religion, society, or culture of the countries they had visited.

Is it possible to convert a *rajasik* wife into a *sattwik* wife? Yes, it is possible. Encouraging her to read the biographies of genuine saints and skillfully persuading her to listen frequently to soothing spiritual music can be of great help. If she can be persuaded to learn how to meditate from a genuine teacher of meditation that will help her immensely. Or if the husband develops genuine interest in spiritual life then the *rajasik* wife may also be gradually inspired to develop similar interest.

(e) How to get along with a *tamasik* wife.

To get along with your *tamasik* wife what you mostly need is extreme patience and tolerance. Being *tamasik,* she will be lazy and often confused. Every now and then, without any valid reason, she may burst into a temper. She will be superstitious and may be easily attracted to crooks masquerading as saints. In this connection I can tell you a sad story. I knew a very dignified American gentleman who held a good position in the US government. But unfortunately his *tamasik* wife suddenly became attracted to a certain pseudo saint and made her husband's life miserable. The husband tried hard to dissuade her from following that questionable spiritual teacher. But she wouldn't listen to any good advice. Eventually they got a divorce.

Divorce is an unfortunate event in married life. Two persons who dearly love each other get united through matrimony. It must be heart-rending to separate themselves from each other through divorce. Yet it is an unpleasant fact that, particularly in the West, a good percentage of marriages end up in divorce. Is it possible to save marriages from divorce? I found an answer to this question from a true story written by Sidney Keegan in her article entitled "Saving A Dying Marriage" published in a Seattle based journal called *Global Vedanta*.[11]

According to the story, Sidney Keegan's hair stylist, a lady in her late fifties, mentioned that she had been married for nearly forty years while all four of her children had been divorced after just a few years of their marriages. Hearing that, Sidney Keegan wondered if the younger generation's attitude toward marriage had anything to do with so many divorces. When asked, her hair stylist said that she also felt that people didn't take marriage as seriously nowadays as they used to do in the past. Now let me quote from Sidney Keegan's article.

---

11. *Global Vedanta*, Vol. 4, No. 1 (Summer 1999) published by Viveka Press, Seattle.

"She (the hair stylist) said, 'living together (without marriage) is too easy, people think that marriage is just a piece of paper. They aren't willing to work at it. It takes a lot of work.'"

Then she said that she and her husband had at one time agreed to separate. They were both unhappy, so her husband wanted to move out. He made the decision just before Thanksgiving, an annual celebration observed in the month of November in the United States. She, however, asked him to wait until the New Year's Day celebration was over, and her husband agreed to that.

She then made up her mind to make sure that she would make his last days with her so comfortable that "he would remember them with pleasure." During that period she served him lovingly and didn't have any expectation from him except to see him happy. She allowed him complete freedom to do whatever made him feel happy and comfortable.

"When the time came for him to leave, he said, 'Why should I leave?'

"From that point on, they were happier than they had ever been before, and never talked of separation again."

The moral of this true story is obvious. The spouses should love each other without any expectations from each other except to make each other happy. This is the secret of saving most marriages from divorce.

(f) How to get along with your husband.

This world is a battlefield. It is full of countless problems. And most of these problems are generated by the conflict between self-interests of people. There are very few people in this world, except those who are saintly, who are capable of giving selfless love.

For example, if your husband is trying to make a living by running his own business, he will never get genuine love from his employees. Or, if he is working as an employee in an office or a company, he will never get genuine love from his boss or his colleagues. That being the case, he can expect genuine love only from his wife. In this world of breakneck competition and perpetual conflict of self-interests, very few people will even give your husband genuine praise or appreciation. Therefore, as his loving wife, it should be your duty to always give him sympathy, love and praise, and never hurt him by any unkind word or criticism. You should make him feel that he is the most important person in your life. This is the secret of how your married life can be made really joyful and happy.

It goes without saying that the husband should do the same for the wife if she happens to be the family's principal bread-winner.

Aside from all this, with the help of your knowledge of the *guna*s you have to assess the nature of your husband. Try to know what *guna* is preponderant in him most of the time. Thus you will come to know whether he is *sattwik*, *rajasik* or *tamasik* by nature. Once you have determined your husband's nature, it will be easier for you to get along with him happily and peacefully.

(g) How to get along with a *sattwik* husband.

If your husband is of *sattwik* nature, you should consider yourself extremely lucky. He will have the characteristics of a person in whom *sattwa-guna* is preponderant most of the time [Please see page 10 to know about these characteristics.] If you are interested in leading a spiritual life, the company of such a husband will help you immensely. Even otherwise, your married life is bound to be peaceful and harmonious if you don't have a strong desire to have a lot of wealth and various kinds of sense enjoyment. Your husband, being of a *sattwik* disposition, will not be interested in all these things.

(h) How to get along with a *rajasik* husband.

If you are of *sattwik* nature there won't be any difficulty in getting along with your *rajasik* husband. He will have all the characteristics of a person in whom *rajo-guna* is predominant most of the time. [Please see pages 12–14 to know these characteristics.] Among other things, he will be very talkative. For example, once during a nearly five and a half hour flight from Seattle to New York I sat in a row just behind an elderly couple. The husband was of *rajasik* temperament and was talking almost non-stop during the entire flight bragging about his business deals, etc. While he was talking to his wife she kept busy knitting something and intermittently saying to her husband, "Yes, dear!" Apparently the couple had been married for many years, and the wife, who was obviously of a *sattwik* temperament, knew exactly how to get along with her *rajasik* husband. Being of *sattwik* nature, she was capable of loving her husband ignoring his minor deficiencies. Had she been of a *rajasik* temperament she would most probably have become irritated and asked her husband to shut up. It should be clearly understood by the readers here that the art of successfully "getting along" with others is not necessarily a strategy to create perfect happiness for those who practice it. But it cannot be denied that using such a strategy can surely make uncomfortable situations tolerable, if not reasonably comfortable.

(i) How to get along with a *tamasik* husband.

I knew a gentleman in India who had the habit of drinking hard liquor a few times a week before going to bed. Any medical book will tell you that alcohol is a depressant. Those who drink alcohol suffer from hangovers. During a hangover the drinker often suffers terribly from mental depression. And such depression is a sure indication that *tamo-guna* has become preponderant in the drinker's body and mind. *Tamo-guna* also causes, among other things, senseless anger. [Please see page 14.]

Due to his hangover, the gentleman would often fly into a rage in the morning and start scolding his wife without any rhyme or reason. His wife was a nondrinker and was of a *sattwik* temperament. After his sudden outbursts of senseless anger, the gentleman would usually leave home and come back an hour or two later when he had cooled off. This would happen when his mind would get over its preponderance of *tamo-guna*. Returning home, he would often apologize to his wife saying that he was sorry for his angry behavior. It went on for many years. Once I asked his wife how she could put up with her husband's frequent outbursts of senseless anger. She replied, "I give no importance to what he says when he scolds me. I think that he is only making some meaningless noise!" This is a great lesson for any wife to learn how she can get along with her *tamasik* husband.

(j) How to get along with your husband in certain family situations.

Some housewives, who are not working women, do not know how to behave with their husbands when they return home from work. When the husbands return home after work, they are usually hungry and may still be occupied with some unresolved problems associated with their work. At that time more blood goes on circulating in their brain. They may then become agitated or angry very easily. Inexperienced wives do not know that this is not the proper time to dump all sorts of domestic problems on their husbands.

For example, as soon as the husband returns home, his wife tells him, "Do you know what *your* son has done today? He has badly dented our new Mercedes car while trying to drive it!" Or, "Our basement is flooded. We now have a serious plumbing problem. You must do something about it right now!"

An experienced and intelligent wife knows that it is better to first give her husband a nice dinner complete with some nice dessert that he likes. By the time he finishes eating his dinner, blood will have come down from his head and started circulating in his stomach. Now he is not likely to be too agitated or angry. This is the right time to talk to him about household problems.

Although I am a monk I have used this technique of calming down the agitated minds of people most effectively more than once. At one time when I was working in the office of our Order's headquarters at Belur Math in India, a gentleman entered our office. He seemed to be quite agitated. I requested him to take his seat, which he did. Then he said angrily, "I have come to you to complain about something. I only wanted to take a few pictures of your temple here. But hardly had I taken a single picture, when one of your watchmen came and very rudely asked me to stop taking pictures. He said to me, 'What kind of a person are you? Can't you read? Are you blind? Didn't you see those big signs telling visitors that photography is prohibited here?' Well, I have come to tell you that I feel extremely insulted at the rude behavior of that watchman. This is a very famous place associated with the memory of Sri Ramakrishna and Swami Vivekananda, why should your employees here behave so rudely with visitors?"

I apologized to him for the rude behavior of the watchman. Then I gave him a plateful of some fruits and sweets that had been offered to the deity at our temple, and asked him to eat. According to Hindu tradition, any food that is offered to the deity is considered very holy. Eating such food is considered spiritually beneficial. By the time the gentleman had eaten those fruits and sweets and drunk a glass of water, some of the blood that was circulating inside his brain had come down to his stomach. He was not that agitated any more.

Then I explained to him why photography was not permitted in our temple. Many devotees come to the temple to meditate there. They feel disturbed when photographers start taking pictures using flash, etc. Aside from that, our non-profit and charitable organization runs only on donations received from some kindhearted and generous people. As we don't have a lot of money and can't pay high salaries to our employees, we are compelled to sometimes employ some less than perfect people as watchmen, etc.

After hearing all this, the gentleman apologized for his own angry behavior and then with folded hands said very humbly, "Swamiji,[12] I wish that all the monks of the Ramakrishna Mission were like you! Please pray for me!"

---

12. "Swamiji" is an honorific expression used to address *sannyasis* or monks (*swamis*) who have taken their final vows of monastic life.

(k) How to get along with jealous and suspicious spouses.

Sometimes either the husband or the wife becomes suspicious about the fidelity of the other spouse. In other words, the husband may suspect that his wife is interested in other men. Or the wife may suspect that her husband is interested in other women. In such a situation the husband must never praise other women in the presence of his wife. Similarly, the wife must never praise other men in the presence of her husband. In addition to that, the husband and the wife should make it a point to attend social events together. None of them must go alone to attend such events. And while attending such social events together, in order to avoid rousing suspicion in the spouse's mind each of them should behave very carefully with the members of the opposite sex.

The cause of such obsessive suspicion or mania is *rajo-guna* overpowered by *tamo-guna*.

(l) How to make up after a quarrel between the husband and the wife.

It is not uncommon for a husband and wife to argue or quarrel sometimes because neither one can claim perfection. But to make up, at least one of the spouses should learn to say to the other, "I am sorry!" or "Please forgive me!" These two sentences can be called "ultimate salvation mantras." They never fail to work. They can resolve most misunderstandings between the husband and the wife.

(m) How to get along with a spouse who suffers from mental illness.

It is extremely difficult to get along with a husband or a wife who suffers from mental illness. The husband or the wife has to make sure that his or her spouse gets good psychiatric treatment.

A very common symptom of mentally ill people is that they do not think that there is anything wrong with them. They don't think that they are mentally ill. Therefore, they cannot be easily persuaded to undergo psychiatric treatment. And if they can somehow be persuaded to go and see a psychiatrist, it is extremely difficult to persuade them to take medication regularly. I have seen quite a few cases where the husband or the wife suffers terribly because the mentally ill spouse stubbornly resists taking medication for his or her mental illness.

To get along with a mentally ill spouse one needs genuine love and patience. I know one gentleman whose wife developed mental illness a few years after their marriage. She could not be easily persuaded to go to the psychiatrist and take medicines. Due to her mental state she could not do her household chores either. Her husband had to step in and do all her work. He was under great mental and physical pressure. Yet he maintained his calm. He told me that he was able to get along with his wife because he remembered all those happy years they had lived together before her illness. He said to me that his wife was then extremely loving and caring towards him.

He said that he was extremely grateful to his wife for her loving care and service during those years. In addition to that, frequently praying to God for her recovery also gave him hope and strength.

CHAPTER 9

HOW TO GET ALONG WITH YOUR FAMILY MEMBERS

(a) How to get along with your children.

According to Chanakya, who is estimated to have lived in India between 350 and 283 B.C., parents should pamper their children until they are five. After that, for ten years they should be put under strict discipline. At age sixteen they should be treated like friends.[13] These instructions apply equally to both sons and daughters.

Getting along with children younger than five needs extreme patience. They are mainly driven by their animal impulses. They lack human intelligence. Judging by percentage, children, who are one year old, have only ten or fifteen percent human intelligence, the remaining ninety or eighty five percent being animal impulse. As they grow, they gradually acquire more and more human intelligence. That's why until they are five, as the wise Chanakya suggests, they should be lovingly pampered and carefully protected from possible harm. Strict

---

13. In Sanskrit: *Lalayet panchavarshani, dasha varshani tadayet. Prapte tu shodashe varshe putram mitravadacharet.*

disciplining will not work that well at this stage. By six years of age most children have acquired enough human intelligence to understand the difference between what is good and what is bad as well as what is helpful and what is harmful. This is the right time to start teaching them through loving but strict discipline how they should shape up to become good persons. This method of teaching should continue until the children are roughly sixteen years old. When they are sixteen they usually have enough percentage of human intelligence to try to make the right decisions for themselves. The parents, who are wiser and more experienced in life, can guide their children now through discussion and proper reasoning as to what they should do.

But above all, parents should try to lead ideal lives in order to be role models for their children. For example, they must neither drink alcohol nor smoke if they want their children to remain free from such harmful addictions.

Nowadays, however, due to the invasion of TV and the internet, children mature into adults much faster. Parents should therefore consider this fact while getting along with their children.

(b) How to get along with married children.

Nowadays, quite a few married sons in many countries seem to defer to their wives.

One evening, a married gentleman in his thirties came to our Vedanta temple in Seattle to talk to me about something important. Around 9 pm, after the conversation, he said to me humorously, "Swami, I must say goodbye to you now. I must hit the road now otherwise I have to spend the night in the doghouse!"

Therefore parents must not say anything against their daughters-in-law in the presence of their married sons. They should not talk against their sons-in-law either in the presence of their married daughters. Also, parents must not give any uncalled for advice to their married sons and daughters concerning their married life or how to bring up their children.

(c) How to get along with your parents and in-laws.

As you grow up you should remember that your parents are your best well-wishers in this world. Therefore, it is in your best interests to follow what they say. Try never to hurt them by your behavior.

After you are married, you must never forget the birthdays of your parents. Make sure to give them your loving greetings and some gifts on their birthdays. You should do the same on Mother's Day and Father's Day. These instructions apply to your behavior in regard to your in-laws as well.

You should remember that your spouse's parents must love your spouse very much. It is natural for them to love you also because you are the husband or wife of their beloved child. So you should treat them like your own loving parents.

(d) How to get along with your relatives.

As mentioned earlier, to get along with your relatives you should first know whether they are *sattwik*, *rajasik* or *tamasik* in temperament and then act accordingly.

CHAPTER 10

HOW TO GET ALONG WITH THOSE WHO ARE NOT MEMBERS OF YOUR FAMILY

(a) How to get along with your friends.

"Who is your true friend?"—Chanakya, also known as Kautilya, who lived in India more than 2,300 years ago, has answered this question.

According to him, a true friend stands by you during your festivities and calamities. He shares his food with you during a famine. He stays by your side during political turmoil or when you have to appear in a court of law. He will also stand by you when you are attending someone's cremation or funeral."[14]

Another book of Hindu wisdom says: "One from whom you cannot even bear the thought of separation is your true friend."[15]

Unfortunately, it is extremely hard to find a friend who

---

14. In Sanskrit: *Utsave vyasane chaiva durbhikshe rashtrabiplave rajadware shmashane cha yah tishthati sa bandhavah.*
15. In Sanskrit: *Atyagah sahno bandhuh.*

can fulfill all these conditions. Therefore, you must consider those who may not be perfect, but are not harmful to you, as your friends and learn how to get along with them.

Hindu tradition teaches, "One should only speak the truth. But one should only speak truths that are pleasant. Unpleasant truths should not be spoken."[16] This teaching is of paramount importance in learning how to get along with your friends. But there are exceptions. Certain special people, such as doctors, parents, teachers, etc, can speak beneficial unpleasant truths under special circumstances. For example, if during check ups doctors find something wrong with their patients' health it is their duty to tell the patients about that. Speaking such unpleasant truths to the patients is the duty of the doctors. Similarly, it is the duty of the parents to speak beneficial unpleasant truths to their children for their children's welfare. But to get along with friends it is always prudent to avoid speaking unpleasant truths to them.

Most people, particularly those who are of *rajasik* temperament, like praise. Therefore, while interacting with your *rajasik* friends you must not point out his or her defects. As nobody is devoid of some good qualities, no matter how few, you should praise those good qualities.

If a friend asks you for a loan, you must give him that loan without expecting its repayment. You should think

---

16. In Sanskrit: *Satyam bruyat, priyam bruyat, na bruyat satyam apriyam.*

that the amount loaned to your friend is your outright gift to him or her. Therefore, while giving such a loan, you should only give such an amount that you can do without. Otherwise, when you ask your friend to repay the loan, you may not only lose your money but also your friend.

It is not wise for you to get involved in the marital problems of your friends. Usually the spouse who is your friend, will accuse the other spouse and talk about his or her defects, real or imaginary. You may give your friend a sympathetic hearing but never say anything negative about the person being accused. It is quite possible that they will make up later, and you will be hated for the negative comments that you made when they were not able to get along with each other.

It is a good practice to talk to your friends about the good qualities and achievements of their children because that will make them happy, but it is not very intelligent to talk to your friends about the good qualities of your own children. If your friends' children are not as bright as your children, talking highly of your own children is likely to make them upset or envious.

It is also not at all a good idea for friends to have a business relationship with each other. Most partnerships between friends turn sour. I knew a person who owned an investment firm. Many of his friends invested their money in his firm. It was that period in America when the stocks of technology companies were yielding very good returns. As a result, those who invested money in their friend's firm earned very good income. And they were very pleased with the performance of their friend who owned the investment firm. Unfortunately, after a while, technology stocks took a nosedive. And those who had invested through their friend's firm lost a lot of money. Then they all blamed the friend who owned the investment firm for their losses. They also started speaking against him to everybody.

Another case. After I became a monk I was attached to one of the *ashrama*s (churches) of our Order in India. There I got to know two gentlemen. One of them was a medical doctor while the other one was a highly placed government officer. Both of them were in their early forties. They were married and had children. Other than being very close friends they were also devotees of Sri Ramakrishna. They were so fond of each other that they decided to live together with their families in the same house. So they bought a very large house jointly in a good neighborhood. But after living together for a year or so in that house, the relationship between these two friends became so strained that they stopped talking to each other. Then they sold the house and started living in two separate houses in two different neighborhoods quite distant from each other.

It is possible that some of your friends may be addicted to drinking alcohol. They may naturally expect you to join them in drinking. For example, when you visit their homes, they may offer you alcoholic drinks. But if you are a nondrinker you may wonder how to refuse without offending their feelings. You won't offend them if you tell them, "I've no prejudice against drinking. But I am sorry, for medical reasons I can't drink. I'll appreciate it if you give me some soft drink or fruit juice, if you have any. Otherwise, just a cup of coffee or tea will do!"

In this connection I can tell you a true story. My elder brother, who was a medical doctor, once went to a city in South India to attend a refresher course in his specialty. At that time he was invited to have dinner at a certain doctor friend's home. No member in our family ever drank liquor, tea or coffee. Nor did anyone smoke tobacco. So my brother said to his friend, "I don't have any prejudice against drinking liquor. But out of respect for my father I don't drink liquor. He was a nondrinker and expected his children to follow his example. It is for this reason I don't drink. If you don't mind, please give me some soft drink instead!" According to my brother, his friend was not the least bit offended.

(b) How to get along with your neighbors.

According to a recent estimate, there are over 311 million people in the United States, while there are approximately 77.5 million pet dogs in America. That's why every day you see many people walking their dogs on the sidewalks in any neighborhood in America. The best method of getting along with those dog-owners is to appreciate their dogs. It is even better if you can remember the names of their dogs. Just as to set yoghurt you have to put a little yoghurt culture in the milk, so also a little friendly inquiry about your neighbor's dog may become the starting point of a friendship between you and your neighbor. You can also ask the neighbor in which block or house in your neighborhood he or she lives.

Our next-door neighbor lives alone and often goes out on pleasure trips to different countries. She has a cat. During her absence she requests us to take care of her cat, which we do. That's how she has become very friendly to us. To get along with neighbors, such good-neighborly behavior can be very helpful.

It is also a helpful habit to greet people with a smile, saying "good morning," etc., when you go out for a walk in your neighborhood or when you go to your neighborhood park to spend a little time there. You should always remember that a smile is very important in getting along with people.

(c) How to get along with powerful people in your society, such as politicians or government officials holding positions of authority.

People who are powerful in society by virtue of their political position or otherwise, are generally *rajasik* people. *Rajo-guna* generates personal worldly ambition and the tendency to dominate over others. If someone surrenders to *rajasik* people when seeking their help, their ego becomes flattered. They try to help and protect those who submit to them. Therefore, those who seek any favor from them should humbly ask for their help.

In this connection I may cite a true incident. The retreat property of our Vedanta Society (church) in Seattle has a small man-made lake. Once some kind of water vegetation started growing and filling up the entire lake. One member of our church who was very knowledgeable about how to get rid of such a problem, asked us to put fish in the lake. He said that fish would then feed on the vegetation and the water of the lake would become clear.

To put fish in our lake, however, we would have to get permission from the Department of Game.[17] Knowing fully well that most people in positions of authority are *rajasik* people, we decided to write a very polite, personal letter to the officer concerned. In that letter we requested him very humbly to help us out of our predicament. We mentioned that we were depending solely on his kindness and help. This worked. We got permission to put fish in our lake without any hassle.

Sri Ramakrishna used to say, "Don't displease people who by virtue of their high positions held in society or government, may have the power to harm you."

(d) How to get along with people who can harm you, if enraged.

It is a well-known fact that *tamo-guna* becomes preponderant in anyone who drinks alcohol. One of the

---

17. Now it is called the Department of Fish and Game.

characteristics of *tamo-guna* is that, among other things, it causes depression. That's why, after drinking a lot of alcohol, one gets a hangover. Aside from this, a preponderance of *tamo-guna* in people also causes senseless anger in them. [See page 14.] People under the influence of alcohol may suddenly become angry without any obvious reason and try to harm you. Therefore Sri Ramakrishna says, "Never enrage a drunken person. Pleasingly address him, if needed, by calling him 'Uncle'." In the West, however, due to the difference in social conditioning, calling someone "Uncle" may not work well. You may address him either as 'Hello, sir' or 'Hello, friend.'

(e) How to get along with people in your workplace.

(*i*) **Getting along with your supervisor or boss:** Usually those who are in supervisory positions also tend to be *rajasik* people. Therefore, always give your supervisor pleasant behavior. You should always greet him with a smile. If he is pleased with your behavior, when the opportunity comes he may promote you. A subordinate official who talks back to his or her supervisor makes a grave mistake. Praise the supervisor frequently, whenever possible. Don't try to give him advice. Nor should it be your duty to correct him.

If you feel like offering a suggestion you should approach him like this: "Sir, you are highly experienced and knowledgeable, I have very little experience, but I have an idea. Will you please see if it is worth anything?"

As mentioned earlier, *rajasik* people try to help and protect those who submit to them. If you want a favor from your *rajasik* supervisor, you should humbly seek his help. He may then go out of his way to help you.

Once a young man who worked in a government office was having difficulty getting along with his supervisor. He came to see me and asked for my advice. Among other things, I asked him to praise his *rajasik* supervisor. Referring to that, he said to me, "Swami, I don't want to flatter anybody!"

Then I said to him, "I am not asking you to flatter your supervisor. Flattery is usually praising the nonexistent qualities of a person. It is as good as lying, and must be avoided. On the other hand, appreciation of the "existent" qualities of a person is not flattery. It is called praise. Everyone in this world must have some good qualities. For example, your supervisor may have beautiful handwriting. You may truthfully say to him, 'Sir, your handwriting is really beautiful. I wish I had such handwriting!' Or he may have put on a new and beautiful suit. If he looks handsome in that suit you can truthfully tell him, 'Sir, it is a beautiful suit!' Such praise will surely make him pleased with you."

(*ii*) **Getting along with your colleagues:** Even though the general rules of how to get along with your friends have to be observed by you in regard to your colleagues at your workplace, you must remember that, just like you, all your colleagues are working for his or her own self interest. They are working there only to earn money for themselves. They are not necessarily your well-wishers or selfless benefactors.

For example, if you get a good promotion most of your colleagues will outwardly congratulate you but inwardly they may be envious and resentful about your promotion. Many of them may think: "This fellow must have got the promotion by somehow flattering the boss! I didn't get the promotion because I don't flatter anybody!"

To get along with these colleagues you should tell them, "In no way am I better than any one of you; I just got lucky. To me, my friendship with you is much more valuable than this promotion. Know that I shall always be your friend and will always need your cooperation. Besides, if it is within my power to help you in anything, just ask for it without any hesitation. That will make me very happy."

I should also mention here that, to deal with colleagues individually on a person-to-person basis, you have to judge them in terms of the *guna* that is predominant in them and act accordingly.

(*iii*) **Getting along with your subordinates:** I have been to Japan many times at the invitation of the Vedanta Society of Japan. While there, I came to know that those who work for a company are expected to have 100% loyalty to that company. Aside from this, there is one protocol that is observed in all offices and companies. The protocol is that when an employee in a subordinate position meets a higher officer, it is his duty to greet the higher officer first. Only then the officer in the higher position is supposed to return his greetings. It is never the other way around. In that connection I would like to narrate an incident that has relevance to the topic that I am discussing here.

Once, when I was in Japan, a Japanese gentleman came to see me. He was a member of the Vedanta Society there. He came to seek my advice in regard to a work-related problem. He said that he was a quality control inspector in a large factory, which manufactured certain kinds of equipment. As a conscientious employee of the company, he needed to make sure that the quality of the equipment manufactured by the company did not fall short of its high standard. As a result, he had to often disqualify the less than perfect products made by the factory workers. That made some of the factory workers unhappy. They stopped greeting the quality control inspector, as they should have done according to protocol. Their behavior naturally upset the gentleman. When he came to see me, he asked, "Swami, what can I do in this situation? I feel insulted when the factory workers behave this way!"

I said to him, "Take it as a challenge. Whether they greet you or not, make it a point to greet them first. Aside from that, as soon as possible, during your lunch hour please invite one of those disgruntled factory workers to have lunch with you. At that time explain to him that like every one else, you also have been working at that company to earn a little money to support your family. Since the company has employed you as its quality control inspector, it is your duty to be loyal to the company and thoroughly examine the quality of all the equipment produced by the company. Therefore, you are duty bound to sometimes disqualify some of the products made by the factory workers. But you do so most reluctantly. You have nothing but good will and sympathy for all the workers."

The gentleman acted upon my advice. He talked with just two or three factory workers, who spread out the message of the quality control inspector among their colleagues and co-workers. As a result, they started greeting the quality control inspector properly.

If you hold a supervisory position and have to deal with quite a few subordinate employees, you should judge their individual nature with the help of your knowledge of the *guna*s.

If you see that a good number of them are *tamasik* by nature it will be hard for you to get good work out of them. Since *tamo-guna* is preponderant in them they will be slow and lazy. Don't give them important things to do.

The subordinates who are *rajasik* by nature, when guided by you properly, can be quite active and helpful, but you have to handle them intelligently. To get the best service out of them, you should watch them carefully, and when they have performed well you should praise and appreciate their work. That will please them.

Being *rajasik* by nature, they will tend to be too talkative. They will also be ambitious and may try to please you through flattery. You should be able to see through such ill-motivated praise and not fall for it.

Rajo-guna, when preponderant in people, scatters their minds. Therefore, due to their scattered minds, they often tend to be forgetful. Very important work that needs 100% attention must not be assigned to them.

Subordinates whose *rajo-guna* is controlled by *sattwa-guna* will prove to be your best workers. [Please see page 17 to know how *sattwa-guna* can use *rajo-guna* to do good things.] They will be efficient, conscientious, and clear thinkers. As their *rajo-guna* is under the control of *sattwa-guna* they will also be active in a helpful way. In spite of that, to initially test them, give them important assignments. If their performance is excellent, you can safely rely on them. After you have tested them, depend on them to have the work done, and they will not disappoint you! They will be your best workers.

(f) How to get along with immigration officers while entering a country.

To get along with the immigration officers well you should be courteous and truthful to them. Never show your temper. For example, during the past 39 years of my stay in the United States I have had to cross the US-Canada border around ten times a year. Every time I would go to Vancouver, stay there for two days, and give

81

some religious discourses there. On the third day I would return to Seattle crossing the same US-Canada border. I used to make all those trips by car. During those border crossings I never had any difficulty in getting along with the immigration officers because I was always courteous and 100% honest with them.

Once by mistake, I left my passport in Seattle, where I live. At the US-Canada border I told the Canadian immigration officer about it. After checking my US driver's license he allowed me to enter Canada. Then he said to me, "Please go to the US immigration office here and tell the officer that you have left your passport by mistake in Seattle. Otherwise, when returning to USA you may have some difficulties."

Following his instruction I went to the immigration officer on the US side. To my surprise the Canadian immigration officer followed me and on my behalf requested the US immigration officer to give me something in writing so that I would be able to enter USA without facing any difficulty at the border.

Another true story. One of my close friends, a university professor, wanted to drive me on my trip from Seattle to Vancouver. His wife also came with us. When we were returning from Vancouver to Seattle we had to stop at the US-Canada border to clear customs and immigration procedures at the US immigration checkpoint. After parking the car we entered the immigration office. An officer came to us and pointing to the three of us asked rather casually, "Where do you *guys* live?"

My professor friend didn't like the officer's manner of questioning. He thought that it was discourteous on the part of the officer to address a lady as a guy. So, pointing to his wife, he said to the officer rather tauntingly, "She is not a guy!"

At this, the officer said to my friend, "Give me your car keys. I will have to check your car." My friend wanted to go with him to the car. But the officer, apparently displeased, said, "No, you all stay here!" Of course nothing was found in the car that was suspicious or objectionable. Later, upon our return to Seattle, we came to know from some of our knowledgeable friends that the immigration officers at the border had such immense power that they can, if needed, even dismantle the car to look for objectionable merchandize or goods such as narcotics, etc.

Another incident. In 1974 our Order sent me from India to work in Seattle in the United States. Our Order's branch in Seattle is known as the Vedanta Society of Western Washington. I came as an assistant to Swami Vividishananda who was the head of that Vedanta Society. He was at that time in his eighties and I was in my early forties. Upon my arrival in Seattle, as I was new to this country, the revered swami said to me, "Swami Vivekananda, the founder of our Order, instructed the monks of our Order to wear western clothes while working in the West." Later he took me to a department store and bought me a very dignified-looking dark blue suit. Then he told me, "This is a nice travelling suit. Use this suit whenever you travel."

Following his advice, for many years I have used that suit while traveling. Over the past 39 years, on invitation, I have travelled numerous times to many countries in just about all the continents. In so doing, I had to fulfill customs and immigration formalities every time I entered the United States. And thanks to revered Swami Vividishananda, in addition to my being very courteous to the immigration officers, it is very likely that my wearing that dignified suit bought by Swami Vividishananda also helped me to be treated well by the US immigration officers. Once, when I arrived in Seattle from a trip abroad, to clear customs I had to stand at the tail end of a long line because my baggage had arrived a little later than that of others. Then an immigration officer came up to me and wanted to know my identity. When I told him who I was, he took me out of the line and asked me to follow him. Then coming to the exit he said, "Reverend, you may go. You don't have to stand in line!" I wonder what in me drew his attention and such kindness. The reason might have been that among all the passengers waiting in line for custom clearance I was the only one wearing a suit!

(g) How to get along with people when you are visiting a foreign country.

Before you go to visit any foreign country it will help you if you learn something about the history and culture of that country. More importantly, you should also know about the manners and customs of the people of that country.

I have been to Japan many times. It is not considered good manners in Japan to touch other people's bodies in public. As in many other Asian countries, exhibiting signs of endearment between men and women in public is also considered highly objectionable in Japan. Once I was going by train from Zushi City to Tokyo. There were many passengers in our coach. Just about all of them were of Japanese nationality. A young American couple—a man and a woman—was also travelling by that coach. Judging by their uniforms I could understand that they belonged to the US Navy. Suddenly they started hugging and kissing each other. As soon as they started behaving that way, I noticed that all the Japanese passengers were gazing down at the floor in order to avoid seeing that embarrassing sight. Those Americans didn't know that what is considered all right in America is considered vulgar in Japan. Had they known it they would have behaved differently.

People of India are not used to using knives and forks while eating their meals. After washing their hands, they eat their meals using their hands and fingers. When travelling in Western countries, they should learn to use forks and knives. Using hands to eat their meals will be considered uncivilized behavior there. They should also learn, among other things, Western table manners while travelling in the Western countries.

Manners and customs differ from country to country. Therefore, before traveling in foreign countries one should get to know the manners and customs of the people of those countries. One should also follow this time-honored advice of Hinduism in regard to human behavior: "Always act according to time, place and the personalities of people." [Please see page 34.]

(h) How to get along with a stranger.

The senior monks of our Order through their years of training acquire the ability to judge people by their *gunas*. That's why most of them know how to get along with strangers and what to expect of them. If you have learnt how to judge a person's nature by his or her *gunas*, it won't be hard for you to get along with even a stranger.

The living room of our *ashrama* (church) in Seattle has several ordinary-looking chairs in it. But among them there is a chair which looks very distinguished. It is so ornate that it looks almost like a throne. It was used by my predecessor, an elderly and highly venerated Swami, who was the founder and spiritual leader (minister) of our *ashrama* called the Vedanta Society of Western Washington. Out of respect for him, a member donated that ornate chair to our Vedanta Society for his use.

One day two young ladies of Western ancestry came to our *ashrama*. It was their first visit to our *ashrama*. I received them cordially at the front door. Then I took them to our living room. One of them, the first one to enter the room, looked around and decided not to sit on the distinguished-looking chair. She chose to sit on an ordinary-looking chair. But the other lady glanced at the chairs and went straight to the distinguished-looking chair and sat on it. Judging by her action I knew that she was a *rajasik* person who sought importance. Being of *rajasik* nature, she was also very talkative. I learned from her that both of them were associated with a large religious group in America, which had roots in India. They had recently left that group because they didn't like its leader. She said that they would like to be members of our Vedanta Society since we believed in the harmony of religions. I told her that they were most welcome to become our members and attend all our activities, such as the weekly discourses, daily vespers, and occasional celebrations. Although I permitted them to be members, I knew that they wouldn't stay with us for long. And my assumption was correct. After associating with us for a few months they quietly left. The reason why they had become members of our relatively smaller church was that the *rajasik* lady wanted to start a similar church of her own. She came to see how we ran our *ashrama*. After they left, one of our long time members who had become somewhat close to those two ladies gave me that information.

In India, within a few minutes of your acquaintance with a stranger you get to know a lot about him or her. Talking to that person you can come to know about the family from which he or she has come, where that person lives, whether he or she is married, and if married, if he or she has got any children. You also get to know about that person's profession, academic qualifications, even his or her salary, etc. Asking questions to know these things is not considered a violation of privacy in India. That's how a stranger within a short time can turn into a friend in India. And getting along with a friend will not be that hard for you. But you must judge that newly-acquired friend by the *guna* that is preponderant in that person. Then it will be possible for you to know how to easily get along with him or her.

In the West, however, it is against etiquette to ask a stranger such probing questions. That will be considered a violation of privacy. Therefore, you should try to guess the nature of a stranger with the help of his or her *guna*s. In the West people are usually of *rajasik* nature. Therefore, to interact with strangers you should observe the guidelines given on pages 35–36 about how to get along with *rajasik* people.

(i) How to get along with the members of your church.

Don't expect to meet perfect people among the members of your church. Those who are already perfect do not need to go to church. The members of your church will naturally be at different levels of spiritual growth. You must not expect saintly qualities in them. To benefit from your association with them you should learn to ignore their defects, if any, and try to see their good sides. Everyone must have some good qualities. To get along with them, praise their good qualities if and when possible. It may also help you immensely if you remember that God does not have any stepchildren. We are all God's true children. Some of the children may be more spiritually exalted than others. But God's love must be all the more for those who are more helpless and need to grow more spiritually.

If your church gives you some voluntary administrative position to supervise certain activities of your church you are likely to encounter some problems. The *Bhagavad-gita*, a famous scripture of Hinduism, rightly says that all human activities and endeavors are fraught with problems, just as fire is always covered by smoke.

It is a custom of the Hindus to put off their shoes before entering a temple. They do that out of respect for God. Therefore, there are designated areas on both sides of the front entrance to the temple to leave shoes. A friend of mine was holding some voluntary supervisory position in a Hindu temple in the United States. He noticed that many devotees would not leave their shoes, as was expected, in the designated areas while entering the temple. There were signs outside the temple instructing the devotees to leave their shoes in the designated areas, but many of them would ignore those signs. As a result, the entrance to the temple would become littered with shoes. My friend couldn't decide how to solve that problem without hurting the feelings of the devotees. Before and after the temple services, he would sometimes use a microphone, reminding devotees that they should put their shoes in the designated areas before entering the temple, but it produced no tangible effect.

So he sought my advice. I instructed him that rather than asking devotees to put their shoes in designated areas he himself should go and start picking up the shoes and put them neatly in the designated areas. This would be another good opportunity for him to serve the Lord. And as soon as he started doing that, other devotees came forward to help him. Thus, in a day or two, the problem was solved and all the devotees started putting their shoes in the designated areas.

This incident teaches us that when we hold voluntary supervisory positions in a church or temple it is not wise for us to try to exercise our authority over other devotees. Instead of doing that, if we try, we can solve the problems humbly and intelligently without hurting the feelings of others.

If you are elected president or become an important office-bearer in a church, it is possible that one or two members may become envious of you. To get along with them, you should try to keep yourself in the background and give them positions of importance whenever possible. For instance, you may request them to introduce or thank dignitaries who on special occasions are invited to speak in your church. In other words, give those disgruntled members the chance to come to the forefront and feel important.

Our church in Seattle used to have a children's pageant

every year as a part of our annual celebration in honor of Sri Sarada Devi, the great woman saint of India. One of our members, an unmarried girl in her twenties, used to organize that children's pageant. After doing that work very efficiently for two or three years, she moved to San Francisco. Thereafter, when two married ladies started organizing the pageant, trouble started.

The main attraction of the pageant was a play in which the children used to play different roles. Some of the children, who were playing important roles in the play, often could not come for rehearsal because their mothers would not bring them regularly to our church. That's why the two ladies in charge of the pageant were forced to give the important roles to their own children. As a result, the other ladies whose children were not given important roles in the play, started accusing those two ladies in charge of the pageant of selfishness and partiality. This created unnecessary friction and unfriendly feelings between the ladies involved in the pageant. When I heard about it, I decided to cancel the children's pageant and replaced it with a humorous skit by adult members of our church. I did that because, according to my understanding, every church is expected to create an environment in which the members can get along with one another joyfully and in friendship.

The above incident teaches us that parents are often blinded by their love for their own children. This blind love or attachment often stands in the way of getting along with other members of the church. Many churches that run Sunday Schools for children encounter similar problems. In such schools the children get along with other children quite well, but not necessarily their parents.

Churches are places where people tend to be trusting and helpful to others. That's why criminals often target churchgoing people as their easy victims. As I am the president of our Vedanta temple in Seattle, once I had to attend a church seminar organized by the police department on how to protect the children of our church members from pedophiles. The police told us that such sex-offenders join churches with ulterior motives and pretend to behave like ideal church members. The church administrators have to keep a watchful eye on them. In case of doubt, they can obtain information from the police department if these members have any criminal history as sex offenders. If that is the case, these members must never be given any opportunity to become close to children. The police also told us that, according to their experience, the nature of these sex offenders cannot be changed by religious sermons or loving behavior from the church members.

(j) How to get along with others in a group-living situation.

To get along with others in a group-living situation, such as in a college dormitory, a monastery or a convent, is not always that easy. How to live peacefully with others in such group-living situations?

Swami Vivekananda used to say that the world, as created by God, is perfect. It is neither good nor bad. The ideas of goodness and badness exist only in our minds. If anything satisfies our self-interest we consider that as good. On the other hand, if something doesn't satisfy our self-interest we consider that as bad. Let me suppose that I am a small businessman but I have a friend who is a multimillionaire. Suddenly I urgently need to borrow $50,000 for my business. I therefore approach my friend to loan me that amount. But I had no idea that he was stingy. He says, "I'm sorry! I wish I could help you, but all my money is tied up in stocks and bonds. Under the circumstances, it is impossible for me to loan you any money." Since my friend is unwilling to help me I consider him a bad friend.

On the other hand had he told me, "Why are you asking me for a loan of $50,000? We have been friends for all these years! I'll give you $100,000 instead. It's not a loan. It's my gift to you. Please accept it," then I would have considered him a very good friend.

The main reason why people cannot live peacefully in group-living situations is that they are selfish. It is their selfishness that makes them see defects in others. Aside from this, people expect others to change and become perfect according to their own ideas of perfection. But the truth is that we cannot change others as much as we want. If we try, we can only change ourselves by becoming less selfish. But we all know that it is extremely hard to give up selfishness.

There is, however, a proven technique to transform selfishness into unselfishness. Selfishness can be transformed into unselfishness through expansion. Potassium cyanide is an extremely potent poison. A single teaspoonful of this poison can kill a human being. But if a teaspoonful of potassium cyanide is dissolved in the water of one of the great fresh water lakes of Canada, it will then be so diluted that it will be completely safe to drink that water. There won't be any poison in that water. So also is the case of selfishness. If individual selfishness can be expanded to include all of humankind it will become as good as unselfishness.

Sri Sarada Devi, a great woman saint of India, gave the same teaching. Once, a lady, known as the mother of Annapurna, came to see Sri Sarada Devi seeking her blessings. At the sight of Sri Sarada Devi she became overwhelmed with emotion and started crying. Sri Sarada Devi said to her, "My child, if you want to have peace, don't see the faults of others. See your own faults. Learn to make the world your own. No one is a stranger, my child, the entire world is your own family!"

Those who live together in a monastery or a convent must always remind themselves of the high spiritual ideal that has drawn them to monastic life. Such remembrance will help them to get rid of their petty faultfinding attitude. They should also remember that those who are already perfect, need not join any monastery or convent. Monasteries and convents are meant only for people who are not perfect, but who want to be perfect.

(k) How to get along with fanatics.

Fanaticism is a kind of mental obsession that may express itself in innumerable ugly forms. In this world, just to name a few, there are fanatics in the areas of religion, politics, health, food, cleanliness, race, sports, environment, etc. To get along with such fanatics is extremely difficult, if not impossible. One should tactfully avoid any confrontation with them. Since they are not amenable to reasoning it is almost impossible to convince them that their way of thinking is wrong. Any effort at changing their fanatical views will only make them angry. As the saying goes, it is never a good idea to wave a red flag at a bull.

Tamo-guna is mainly responsible for such fanaticism. When *tamo-guna* becomes prominent in people's minds their sense of reasoning becomes clouded by confused thinking. Only such people can easily turn into fanatics. It is they who can kill innocent people in the name of religion or politics, or take part in racial or religious riots.

(l) How to get along with those who are critically ill in a hospital.

It is always a good idea to visit them frequently and tell that you love them and you are praying to God for their recovery. It is, however, not a good idea to tell them that they are looking very well as some inexperienced visitors who come to visit such patients in the hospital often say to them. If the patients are not feeling well such words will never be able to cheer them up. However, holding their hands occasionally, if the situation permits, can give them some comfort. If the patient asks, "What do my doctors say? Do they say that I'll be cured?" say to the patient, "I haven't talked to your doctor, but I'm sure that you will be cured. Doctors in this hospital are very well trained and experienced. You can fully rely on them. Aside from this, so many people, who love you, have been praying to God for your recovery. Surely God will grant their prayer! I'm sure, by God's grace, you will be cured soon."

(m) How to comfort the bereaved.

The husband of one of my elder sisters was a government officer in West Bengal in India. He was renowned for his efficiency and honesty. Therefore, the government promoted him to a higher position. Before handing over charge to his successor, he discovered that the accountant of his office had defalcated a substantial sum of government money in collusion with the cashier. As he was going to report it to the government, the accountant privately engaged some goons to murder him. The goons stealthily entered his home at night and killed him in the presence of my sister, who being unarmed could offer no resistance. The younger brother of my sister's husband was a teacher in a college run by our monastic order near Calcutta. Immediately after this mishap, he came and took my sister and her two young daughters for their safety to his stuff quarters provided by the college. At that time I was a young swami stationed at the headquarters of our Order near Calcutta. A very senior swami, who was in charge of the branch of our order that ran that college, called me and said, "Your sister is extremely sad and depressed at her husband's death. It may help if you please come and try to comfort her." So, with the permission of the headquarters, I went to see her. Never before had I faced any occasion when I had to comfort anyone who was bereaved. So I had no idea about how to comfort my sister. Then I remembered a teaching of the ancient Hindu sage Patanjali. To get rid of negative thoughts he advised us to take the help of positive thoughts. He called this technique *pratipaksha-bhavanam*. According to this technique, sad thoughts could only be counteracted by thoughts of happiness. Similarly, thoughts of anger and hatred could be counteracted by thoughts of love.

Therefore, when I went to my sister I decided to talk to her only about happy things.

I mostly talked about those happy days when we were growing up at home together. After I had talked that way for an hour or so she could even smile remembering some of my childhood pranks. I made it a point not to talk at all about the good qualities of her deceased husband or how good a person he was, because that would have made her miss him all the more. The technique of *pratipaksha-bhavanam* helped me comfort my bereaved sister immensely. I would therefore advise the readers to use this technique to comfort bereaved people. To comfort the bereaved, many make the grave mistake of praising or talking highly about the good qualities of the deceased person. Since the bereaved people miss the deceased person very much, such words of praise for the deceased person only increase their sadness and sorrow by aggravating their sense of loss.

But there can be a few exceptions. For example, if some have lost their *very elderly* parents it may not be a bad idea to talk to the bereaved sons or daughters about the good qualities of their departed parents. The words of praise for the departed parents will surely minimize the grief of such people. The awareness of the probability of death of near and dear ones in old age minimizes the sense of loss when elderly relatives die of natural causes. However, in case of violent deaths of such elderly relatives the sense of loss is likely to be very acute. In such a situation the technique of *pratipaksha-bhavanam* should be used.

(n) How to get along with politicians.

It is a fact that most politicians get involved in politics motivated by self-interest. And most of them, if not all of them, are *rajasik* by nature. Being *rajasik*, they have a craving for name, fame, power and position. Politicians who occupy important positions have the power to either help or harm others. Therefore, to get along with them one has to be extremely tactful and cautious. It is not at all a good idea for an ordinary citizen to antagonize them.

(o) How to deal with a person who tries to insult you.

There is a saying in India: "You must learn to ignore the words of those who try to insult you. Their words can't burn you and give you blisters!"

People can insult you only when you allow yourself to be insulted. Nobody can insult a person who is determined not to feel insulted. For example, once a person said to another, "You're no better than a donkey!"

The other person responded, "Hush! Hush! Let me look around and make sure that there is no donkey here. Otherwise, it will feel insulted because I am much worse than a donkey!" It is obvious that it is not easy to insult a person who is determined not to feel insulted.

Another example. An impolite atheist once said to a Hindu monk, "I think you are a crook!" The monk smiled and said, "That's all right, but I don't yet bite anybody. Please come, let's sit and drink some tea together!"

In order not to feel insulted, one should develop a keen sense of humor and also some humility. Saints have genuine humility. They don't think that they are superior to others. They are not even aware of their saintliness. That's why they don't feel insulted.

There are many in this world who want to feel superior.

To feel superior they buy expensive waterfront homes, acquire expensive cars, join exclusive clubs, try to gain high political positions, etc. If we think a little we discover that only those who are convinced of their own inferiority want to feel superior. Therefore, in trying to feel superior they unknowingly display their inferiority. Those who are *really* superior don't want to feel superior. Humility, which is a common characteristic of saints, is not a sign of low self-esteem. On the contrary, it is the sign of true superiority.

Aside from all this, we feel insulted by the words of others because we give them undue importance. Once, when I was sitting in the community-dining hall of our temple, a tiny little boy came to me and said, "You are a monster!" I didn't at all feel insulted by his words. On the contrary I thought that what he had said was very cute. I also knew that children of his age in America were very fond of watching that TV show for young children called "Sesame Street." A character in that show is a muppet named Cookie Monster, who is very fond of eating cookies. So I asked him, "Am I the Cookie Monster?" He immediately said, "Yes!" Then I asked someone in the dining hall to give the boy a cookie, and that made him exceedingly happy!

From the perspective of God-knowing saints and prophets most people are like so many cute children. They have yet to grow up spiritually. That's why saints neither take offence nor feel insulted or hurt at the behavior of such people. For example, Jesus while on the cross said to God about his persecutors, "Father, please forgive them because they don't know what they are doing!"

(p) How to get along with those who try to cheat you.

Swami Vivekananda once said, "In the middle ages, there were robbers, now more cheats. " He made this statement at the turn of the 19th century. We can safely presume that the number of cheats has only become larger in this 21st century.

Cheats have always been there. Nearly two thousand years ago Jesus warned his followers about false prophets. Even in Sanskrit, an ancient language several thousand years old, we find counterparts of the English word "cheat," such as *pravanchaka* and *prataraka*.

Nowadays in just about every sphere of human activity you may encounter cheats. And there is no glory in being cheated by others. Only those who lack intelligence get cheated. Hindu scriptures teach that only the trustworthy should be trusted. While the scriptures encourage helping the poor and the needy with money, food, etc., they also instruct that such help should be given only to those who *really* deserve such help.

One young man who was a member of our Vedanta temple in Seattle, had to go downtown for some work. There a street person approached him and begged for some money, saying that he was hungry and needed to buy food. That young man said to him, "Come with me.

I shall buy food for you." After buying some food, he handed the sack of food to the street person and walked away. After walking only a short distance, he looked back and saw the street person dumping the entire sack of food into a garbage can. Obviously, the street person had asked for money not to buy food, but to buy drugs or alcohol. This is an example of why Hinduism instructs its followers to give gifts to only those who deserve them.

At one time in the past the word "savior" used to mean great spiritual teachers like Sri Krishna, Buddha and Jesus. Now, to speak humorously, the great saviors of the world are the department stores, and other shops that sell various consumer goods. If you go to any shopping mall in the United States you will encounter big signs placed in front of these shops claiming how much money you can *save* by shopping there! My friends tell me that storeowners first jack the prices of merchandise up 100%. Then they give the shoppers a seemingly large discount, say 30%! This is how the shoppers are fooled and cheated by them.

Businesses are run to generate profit for the owners. They are not run to save your money! There are some large department stores in the US where, if you enter, you may not find any exit signs to help you come out of the stores. This is deliberately done with the hope that when the shoppers are made to go round and round inside the stores, they are more likely to be attracted by the merchandise that are on display there. Thus the shoppers end up buying some unnecessary things that they have to get rid of eventually through garage sales and Craig's List!

Some chemical compounds that absorb moisture from the atmosphere, are called hygroscopic. The stores in US sell bath soaps that claim to be hygroscopic. They are supposed to absorb moisture from the atmosphere and moisturize the skin of the users. For example, glycerin is hygroscopic. When soap is manufactured, glycerin is also produced along with it as its byproduct. Glycerin is then carefully separated from soap because, glycerin being hygroscopic, its presence in soap would make the soap melt. Calling a solid cake of bath soap a moisturizer or hygroscopic is a lie that is used by some soap manufacturing companies to fool buyers.

In addition, some companies manufacture so-called glycerin soaps. Glycerin is hygroscopic and cannot be present in solid soap. Had that been the case, the soap would be in a liquid state, not solid. The so-called glycerin soap is called "transparent soap" in chemistry. By treating soap with ethyl alcohol transparent soap is manufactured. Such soap does not have any moisturizing quality.

You may wonder how you can save yourselves from these cheats. The only things that can save you are your keen intelligence and sense of reasoning. When you have a preponderance of *sattwa-guna* your intelligence becomes very keen. With its help you can judge people, places and situations correctly, and act accordingly. You can't be cheated by anyone at that stage. A keen sense of reasoning is also an effective armor against the designs of cheats and swindlers.

There are some people who think that using their judgement about others is not a sign of true spirituality. They think that trusting everybody without discrimination is a great virtue. But Sri Ramakrishna, considered one of the greatest saints of this age by Hindus, taught his followers that it is not a spiritual quality to indiscriminately trust everybody. Once a disciple of Sri Ramakrishna named Yogin bought a cooking pan from the market. It was discovered later that the pan was defective. It had a crack in it. When asked, Yogin said that, since he trusted the seller, he didn't think of checking the pan thoroughly before buying it. Thereupon Sri Ramakrishna said to Yogin, "Be a good devotee of God, but don't be a fool!"

(q) How to get along with your students.

Once, on invitation, I had to give a talk to a group of high school teachers in a city in Washington State. During my talk I said to them, "Let us consider a hypothetical situation. Let us suppose that a student is finding it very hard to solve a math problem. So he goes to his math teacher seeking his help. The teacher is very friendly and always willing to help his students. He glances at the problem and says reassuringly to the student, 'It's quite easy to solve this problem. I'll show you how to do it!' Then the teacher helps the student solve the math problem.

Now my question to all of you is this: "Is this teacher a

good teacher?"

All the teachers who were listening to me said that the math teacher was good because he was very friendly and was able to help the student. Then I told them that their judgment was not correct. The math teacher was not a good teacher because he destroyed the self-confidence of the student. He should not have said to the student that the problem, which was very difficult to the student, was easy to solve. Had he been a really good teacher he should have said, "It's indeed a difficult problem. Let's see if we can solve it!"

Teachers cannot infuse knowledge into students' minds. They can only trigger the functioning of the learning mechanism that's in the students' minds. When a teacher destroys the self-confidence of the students, he does the worst harm to them. Swami Abhedananda, a spiritually illumined saint of the Ramakrishna Order of India, used to rightfully say, "Education is the manifestation of knowledge already in man." Teachers can only help the students to manifest the knowledge which is already present in them. This manifestation of knowledge is no other than the acquisition of knowledge.

Ancient scriptures of Hinduism speak of *shraddha* as an essential ingredient in the acquisition of any kind of knowledge—spiritual or secular. From the teacher's standpoint, *shraddha* means the teacher's confidence in the ability of the student to acquire knowledge. Then again, from the student's standpoint, *shraddha* means the student's confidence in the teacher's ability to help him acquire knowledge.

If the students don't have *shraddha* for their teachers they won't be able to learn anything with the help of their teachers. For the students there are two kinds of teachers—*direct* teachers and *indirect* teachers. Indirect teachers are the authors of textbooks that the students have to study. In regard to both kinds of teachers, students must have *shraddha.*

In addition to having *shraddha,* the teachers must have the ability to make difficult subjects understandable to the students. They should have the ability to come down to the level of understanding of their students and teach accordingly. Using difficult words and expressions, they need not make a display of their pedantry to impress their students.

Once, in India, before I became a monk, I had to tutor a student who had been preparing for her high school graduation examination. I had been requested by her father to tutor her because he thought that she was a mediocre student and needed to improve. After I had tutored her for about six months her results turned out to be so excellent that her father was surprised. He asked me, "How did you do it?" I replied, "Just by increasing her self confidence through encouragement!"

That student later graduated from the university and became an officer in the audit department of the government of India.

(r) How to get along with your guests.

The Taittiriya Upanishad, an ancient scripture of Hinduism, teaches that a guest should be treated like a God. A guest should be treated with great honor and given the most cordial hospitality. In this age, however, that instruction is not literally followed by most Hindus. Nevertheless, extending hospitality to guests is still considered a very important aspect of Hindu life. But this does not appear to be true for all people. An American friend of mine once humorously said, " Fish and visitors stink after three days!" This being the attitude of some people in the world, it might be helpful for them to learn about hospitality in the Hindu tradition.

There are many stories in the Hindu scriptures emphasizing the glory of hospitality. *The Mahabharata* tells us the story of King Yudhishthira. Once the king performed a ritual called *ashwamedha yajna*. As a part of that ritual, he had invited hundreds of Brahmin priests and monarchs of different kingdoms. King Yudhishthira treated them with great hospitality.

After they had left, a mongoose with a golden colored head came to the court of King Yudhishthira and said, "The lavish hospitality extended by King Yudhishthira to all these people during the *ashwamedha yajna* is nothing compared to the hospitality of a dirt poor Brahmin who lived in the holy place Kurukshetra.

"Due to a terrible famine in that area, whatever food the poor Brahmin had in his home was completely ex-

107

hausted. He and the other members of his family had not eaten any food for days and were starving. All of them had become very weak and emaciated. With great effort, however, the Brahmin was finally able to procure some oats. Toasting it and grinding it into flour his wife made a small quantity of *shaktu*[18]—a simple food that the poor in India sometimes eat. After his daily worship of God, when the Brahmin was about to have his meal along with his family, a guest arrived.

"The guest, also a Brahmin, was quite hungry. The poor Brahmin received the guest with due respect and honor. Then he gave the guest his own share of food to eat. But it was not enough to satisfy the guest's hunger. So the poor Brahmin's wife insisted that her share of *shaktu* also be given to the guest. But that didn't appease the guest's hunger either. Then one by one the poor Brahmin's son and the daughter-in-law also gave their shares of food to the hungry guest. After eating all their food, the guest was well pleased and revealed his true identity.

"He was no other than *Dharma*, the deity of righteousness. The deity had taken the form of that guest to test the poor Brahmin's spirit of hospitality. The deity blessed all the members of the Brahmin's family. Then, as a reward for their wonderful spirit of hospitality, a heavenly chariot came down for them and took all of them to *brahmaloka*."

18. In North India it is now called *chhatu*. This name is derived from its ancient Sanskrit name *shaktu*.

Hidden inside its hole, the mongoose witnessed this wonderful event. It felt that the extraordinary hospitality of the Brahmin's family and their self-sacrifice had transformed their home into a holy and sacred shrine. With a deep feeling of respect and admiration the mongoose started rolling on the floor of that home. While doing so it rubbed its head against some traces of *shaktu* that were lying on the floor. As a result, the mongoose's head miraculously attained a beautiful golden hue.

Hoping that King Yudhishthira's lavish hospitality must have rendered the place where the *ashwamedha yajna* had been performed equally holy, the mongoose rolled on that ground. He had hoped that such an act would color his entire body gold, but nothing like that happened. So the mongoose concluded that the hospitality of the poor Brahmin of Kurukshetra was far superior to that of King Yudhishthira.

This story in *the Mahabharata* gives us an idea of what ideal hospitality is in the Hindu tradition.

(s) How to get along with your servants.

In economically developed countries only a rare few rich people can employ servants, cooks, gardeners, etc. But in developing countries many middle class people can employ cooks and servants in their homes. It is necessary for such people to know how to get along with their servants. In the state of West Bengal in India mostly Bengali-speaking people live. They call their maidservant *jhi* (pronounced jhee). The meaning of the word *jhi* is "daughter," indicating that she is supposed to be a member of the family.

On invitation I have visited Brazil many times. During those visits, I had to stay a few times as a guest in the home of a very hospitable Brazilian lady. She belonged to the upper middle class and lived in her spacious home near the city of Brasilia. Her house had a sizable garden. One married young man was her gardener. With his wife and very young son the gardener lived in the quarters provided by the owner on the same property. The owner also had a maidservant and a cook. She treated her employees with much love and kindness. She behaved with them as if they were members of her own family. She seemed to love the gardener's little son as though he was her own grandson. In the dining hall the maidservant and the cook would eat together with her and the guests. While I stayed at her home as her guest, she would refer to her employees as "friends." She is a perfect role model for those who want to learn how to get along with their cooks and servants.

(t) How to get along with saints.

One may think that getting along with saints or saintly people should be quite easy. But it is not true. Ramdas Kathia Baba, a famous 19th century Hindu saint of Vrindaban, used to say, "Saints are like elephants. Elephants have two kinds of teeth—their tusks, and the teeth inside their mouths to chew their food. People can see the tusks but not those inner teeth." Similarly, saints have two personalities—the outer and the inner. Ordinary people can see only their outer personality. They cannot see the inner personality of saints. That's why it is difficult for them to judge saints.

Saints being spiritually illumined always have a preponderance of *sattwa-guna* in them. Yet, outwardly they may sometimes appear to be sleepy. Such sleepiness is not an indication of preponderance of *tamo-guna* in them. It is caused by their natural *sattwik* tendency to go within and remain immersed in the thought of God.

Aside from this, many saints owing to their natural humility like to hide their saintliness from others because they do not want to be adored by anybody. An example of this we find in the life of Sri Ramakrishna.

Vijay Krishna Goswami, a renowned leader of the Brahmo Samaj (church), was one of the closest admirers of Sri Ramakrishna. When Vijay lived in Calcutta, off and on he would come to see Sri Ramakrishna in Dakshineswar, a suburb of Calcutta. For a while, in connection with his work, Vijay had to move to Dacca, a city several hundred miles away from Calcutta.

While in Dacca, he had a strange experience. When Sri Ramakrishna was still in Dakshineswar, Vijay saw Sri Ramakrishna appear before him in Dacca. To make sure, Vijay even touched Sri Ramakrishna's body at that time. According to Yoga scriptures, perfected yogis have the power to be simultaneously present in different places.

Some days later when Vijay came to see Sri Rama-krishna in his small room in Dakshineswar, he narrated that incident to a young man named Narendra who was present there. Overhearing that conversation, Sri Rama-krishna said to Vijay with a smile, "Whom you saw there must have been someone else!"

These words of Sri Ramakrishna apparently puzzled Vijay. But Narendra called Vijay aside and told him that Sri Ramakrishna had also miraculously appeared before him a few times in his bedroom at his Calcutta home, and given him spiritual instructions. Sri Ramakrishna didn't want to impress anybody by his yogic powers and acquire any kind of fame. Therefore he didn't want the news of that Dacca incident to go around. This is why he humorously tried to make light of what Vijay had said about that incident.

It is not possible for others to judge a saint's action by seeing his external behavior. Once Swami Turiyananda, a spiritually illumined swami of the Ramakrishna Order, was sitting with another person in the courtyard of the monastery. A young monk at that time was about to en-ter the shrine room of the monastery. Suddenly, without any obvious reason, Swami Turiyananda gave the young monk a severe scolding. After the scolding, he asked the monk to go to the shrine.

The person who was sitting next to Swami Turiyananda asked the swami, "Why did you scold that monk?" Swa-mi Turiyananda replied, "When the monk was about to enter the shrine I could see some negative thoughts coming to his mind. That's why I scolded him. My scolding startled him and helped him get rid of those thoughts!"

Hindu scriptures mention that a spiritually illumined saint may sometimes behave outwardly like a child, a ghoul or a mad man. Saints use their outer personalities as so many disguises to hide their saintliness from others. That's why it is very difficult to recognize a genuine saint by his external appearance or behavior. Nevertheless, if anyone happens to be in the company of a genuine saint that person becomes spiritually benefited.

Hindu scriptures teach that the minds and bodies of all human beings contain an extremely subtle substance called *tanmatra*s. Being extremely fine, *tanmatra*s are invisible.

Every human being can be compared to a fragrant flower. Following the principle of divisibility of matter, the fragrant substance in a flower surrounds it like a fine mist. When we bring our noses within that mist we get the fragrance.

Similarly, all human beings emit *tanmatra*s that form a fine mist of *tanmatra*s around them. *Tanmatra*s represent the personalities of people. Tanmatras emitted by a *sattwik* person will have the characteristics of *sattwa-guna*, while a *rajasik* or *tamasik* person's *tanmatra*s will have the characteristics of *rajo-guna* or *tamo-guna*. For that reason, the *tanmatra*s emitted by the saints are very holy and pure. Those who come within the mist of their *tanmatras* become spiritually benefited. That's why scriptures encourage spiritual aspirants to have holy company. Although it is difficult to judge saints by their outer appearance or behavior, their company nonetheless will help anyone who can come close to them.

CHAPTER 11

CONCLUSION

Only perfect people can interact with others perfectly.

The purpose of writing this book was to give a few guidelines to average people about how to get along with others. Getting along with others does not mean establishing a perfect relationship with others. They are only techniques to make a situation better.

In this world every person's mind is different from the minds of other people. Then again, a person is more his or her mind than the body. And the only function of a conscious mind is thinking.

No thought, however, is ever lost. Every thought gets stored in the subconscious domain of our mind. The mind is like a lake. All the past thoughts get accumulated at the bottom of that lake which is the subconscious domain of our mind. Such submerged thoughts at the subconscious level are called *samskara*s in Sanskrit. It is possible to retrieve them from the subconscious level and bring them up again to the conscious level. This process is called remembering or recollecting.

When a person's mind is in a state of preponderance of

sattwa-guna his thoughts will have all the characteristics of that *guna*. Serenity, calmness, selflessness, sympathy, unselfish love, kindness, compassion, love of God, lack of egoism, humility, etc., will become manifest in that mind. Then again, in a state of preponderance of *rajo-guna*, that same mind will have all the characteristics of *rajo-guna* in it. Restlessness, selfishness, greed, anger, lustfulness, egoism, the tendency to dominate over others, etc., will become manifest in that mind. Similarly, in a state of preponderance of *tamo-guna* all the characteristics of that *guna*, such as confusion, senseless anger, lustfulness, depression, etc., will become manifest in the mind.

Since at any given point in time each *guna* tries to make itself predominant by subduing the other two, the mind keeps on changing. That's why there is fluctuation in human behavior. The same person may behave differently at different times.

Borrowing mathematical terms we can call each of these thoughts a vector. If most of the vectors in a certain person's mind are of *sattwik* nature, then the resultant of these vectors will be a *sattwik* personality. Therefore, every person has to make effort to think *sattwik* thoughts all the time. To make such thinking possible, one should also take *sattwik* food and drink that are conducive to creating a state of preponderance of *sattwa-guna* in one's body and mind.

Only such *sattwik* people are capable of correctly judging other people with the help of common sense and the knowledge of the *guna*s. This capability enables them to get along with other people more easily than what *rajasik* or *tamasik* people can do.

It is also mentioned in the Hindu scriptures that a mind with a preponderance of *sattwa-guna* enables a person to experience God. A mind, which has preponderance of *sattwa-guna*, is also called a pure mind. The echo of this ancient teaching of Hinduism we find in Christianity also when Jesus says, "Blessed are the pure in heart for they shall see God." Aside from this, perfection is just another name for God.

Sattwik people have a realistic view of the world. They realize that it is not possible for them to change others and make them perfect. They also realize that, if they try, they can only change themselves and make themselves perfect. So they learn to adjust to this less than perfect world, and while striving for individual perfection, try to get along with others following the path of unselfishness and self-sacrifice. In this manner, *sattwik* people gradually manifest their inherent divinity and perfection and attain sainthood. It is they alone who can get along with others without hurting anybody. They alone can love their enemies because they don't see enemies anywhere. They see divinity in everything and in every being. The following parable of Sri Ramakrishna (1836-1886) beautifully depicts such a saintly soul.

"There was a monastery in a certain place. The monks residing there went out daily to beg their food. One day a monk, while out for his alms, saw a landlord beating a man mercilessly. The compassionate monk stepped in and asked the landlord to stop. But the landlord was filled with anger and turned his wrath against the innocent monk. He beat the monk till he fell unconscious on the ground. Someone reported the matter to the monastery. The monks ran to the spot and found their brother lying there. Four or five of them carried him back and laid him on a bed. He was still unconscious. The other monks sat around him sad at heart; some were fanning him. Finally someone suggested that he should be given a little milk to drink. When it was poured into his mouth he regained consciousness. He opened his eyes and looked around. One of the monks said, 'Let us see whether he is fully conscious and can recognize us.' Shouting into his ear, he said, 'Revered sir, who is giving you milk?' 'Brother,' replied the holy man in a low voice, 'He who beat me is now giving me milk.'"[19]

That monk had attained perfection. That's why he experienced divinity everywhere. For him interacting with anyone was like interacting with God.

---

19. Quoted from *The Gospel of Sri Ramakrishna* by Swami Nikhilananda.

GLOSSARY

Advaita **philosophy:** A branch Hinduism that speaks of God as the impersonal and formless Divine Reality that transcends time, space and causation.

Antahkarana: The inner instrument that helps us to know things. Although a technical word, it roughly means the mind.

Bhakti: Loving devotion to God.

Bhakti Yoga: The Path of Love; one of the four fundamental types of spiritual discipline.

Brahmachari: In Hinduism, a religious novice.

Buddhi: The determinative faculty of the *antahkarana* inadequately translated as "intellect."

Chanakya: A Hindu wise man who lived about 2300 years ago. He was advisor to the Maurya emperor Chandragupta.

Divine Mother: God looked upon as mother.

Divine Mother Kali: One of the many names of the Divine Mother.

Guna: Property or characteristic trait; any of the three subtle substances that constitute *prakriti* or Mother Nature. According to *Sankhya* philosophy, *prakriti* consists of three *guna*s known as *sattva*, *rajas*, and *tamas*. *Tamas* stands for inertia or dullness, *rajas* for activity or restlessness, *sattwa* for balance, harmony and righteousness.

Hinduism: One of the most ancient of the major religions. It is practiced mainly in India.

Kapila: An ancient Hindu sage; founder of the *Sankhya* school of philosophy.

Kautilya: Same as Chanakya.

Manu: The ancient sage and lawgiver of Hinduism.

***Manas*:** A function of the *antahkarana* inadequately translated as "mind."

Patanjali: A renowned sage of ancient India who lived in the 2nd Century BC. He is the founder of the Yoga system of Hindu philosophy and the author of the *Yoga Sutras*.

***Prakriti*:** Primordial Nature, in association with *Purusha*, creates the universe. It is one of the categories in the school of *Sankhya* philosophy.

***Purusha*:** (lit., a man): A term of *Sankhya* philosophy denoting the eternal Sentient Principle. According to *Sankhya* there are many *Purusha*s.

***Rajasik* person:** A person in whose body and mind *rajo-guna* is preponderant most of the time.

Rajo–guna: *see Guna.*

Ramakrishna (Sri Ramakrishna): A 19th century Hindu saint (1836-1886) known as the saint of the harmony of religions; also regarded as a Divine Incarnation by many.

Ramakrishna Order: A philanthropic organization in India named after Sri Ramakrishna and founded by Swami Vivekananda in 1897.

***Samskaras*:** Impressions of past thoughts.

Sankhya philosophy: The most ancient school of philosophy in India.

Sattwa–guna: *see Guna.*

***Sattwik* person:** A person in whose body and mind *sattwa-guna* is preponderant most of the time.

Shraddha: Implicit faith in one's teacher or other respected people.

Swami: An ordained Hindu monk who has taken his final vows of renunciation.

Swami Vivekananda (1863-1902): The foremost disciple of Shri Ramakrishna and the founder of the Ramakrishna Order of monks and the Ramakrishna Mission. He was the first to effectively preach Hinduism in the West. A great orator, he was the star speaker at the Parliament of Religions held in Chicago in 1893.

***Tamasik* person:** A person in whose body and mind *tamo-guna* is preponderant most of the time.

Tamo–guna: *see Guna.*

Tanmatras: The elementary constituents of the universe. Tanmatras are extremely subtle.

Vidya-shakti: A term used by Sri Ramakrishna for wives who help their husbands advance in their spiritual lives.

INDEX

About the Author

Swami Bhaskarananda was born and educated in India and joined the Ramakrishna Order as a monk in January 1958. Before coming to Seattle in 1974, he was attached to the Headquarters of the Order at Belur (near Calcutta) for 13 years. He has been President of the Vedanta Society of Western Washington in Seattle since 1980. He is also the spiritual head of the Vedanta Society of Hawaii and the Vedanta Societies in Vancouver and Calgary in Canada. On invitation, the Swami has traveled extensively in the United States, Canada, Brazil, Argentina, Uruguay, England, France, Japan, Iceland, and the Netherlands, giving talks on Hinduism and other spiritual topics. He has also visited China, Russia, New Zealand and Australia. He is a founding member and past President of the Interfaith Council of Washington State (now called The Interfaith Network) and was an Interfaith Partner in the Church Council of Greater Seattle. The Swami is the author of seven other books, several of which have been translated into other languages including Dutch, Kannada, Portuguese, Spanish, and Telugu. He is also the founder and editor-in-chief of the quarterly journal *Global Vedanta*.